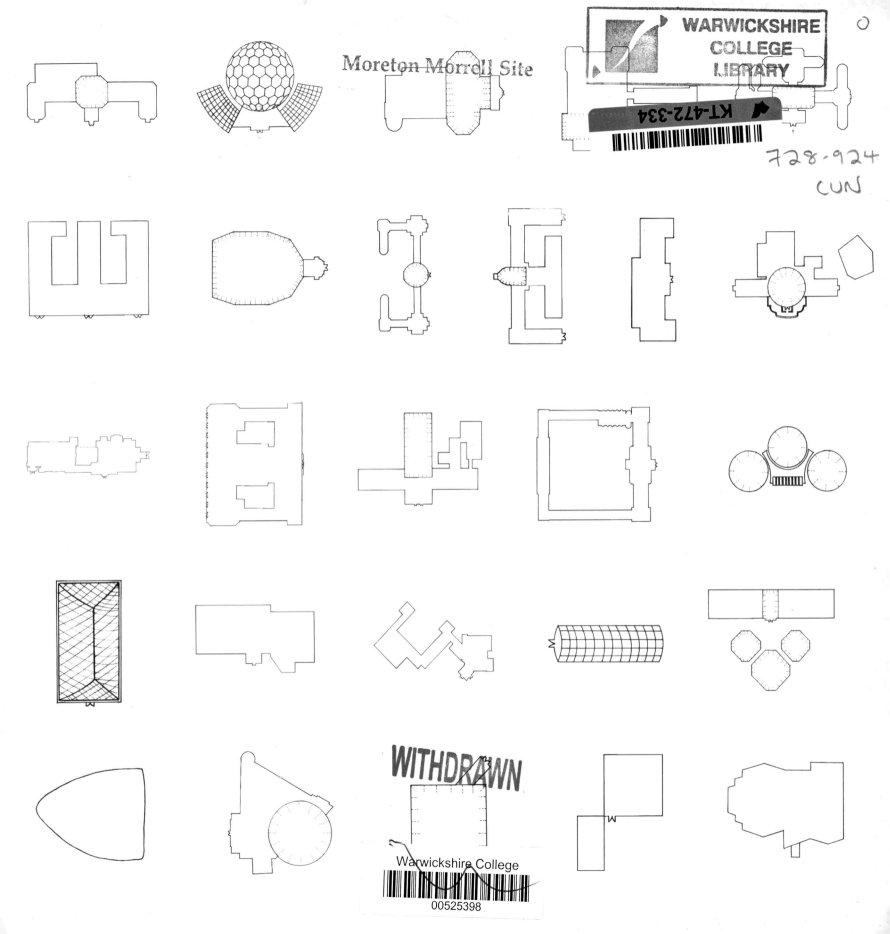

CRYSTAL PALACES

CRYSTAL PALACES

GARDEN CONSERVATORIES OF THE UNITED STATES

Anne S. Cunningham

PRINCETON ARCHITECTURAL PRESS   NEW YORK

Princeton Architectural Press

37 East 7th Street

New York, NY 10003

212.995.9620

For a free catalog of other books published by Princeton Architectural Press, call toll
free 1.800.722.6657 or visit www.papress.com

Frontispiece: Crystal Bridge Tropical Conservatory, courtesy of Myriad Botanical Gardens

Cover: Enid A. Haupt Conservatory, photo by Kay Wheeler, courtesy of The New York
Botanical Garden

Project Editor: Beth Harrison

Design: Adam B. Bohannon

Acquiring Editor: Jan Cigliano

Conservatory plans on endpapers: Whitney Kellogg

Special thanks to Ann Alter, Amanda Atkins, Eugenia Bell, Jane Garvie, Caroline
Green, Mia Ihara, Clare Jacobson, Leslie Ann Kent, Mark Lamster, Anne Nitschke,
Lottchen Shivers, Jennifer Thompson, and Deb Wood of Princeton Architectural Press
    —Kevin C. Lippert, Publisher

Library of Congress Cataloging-in-Publication Data

Cunningham, Anne S.

Crystal palaces : garden conservatories of the United States / Anne S.
Cunningham.

p. cm.

Includes bibliographical references and index.

ISBN 1-56898-242-9 (alk. paper)

1. Conservatories—United States. I. Title.

NA8360 .C86 2000

728'.924'0973—dc21

00-008825

Printed and bound in Italy

04 03 02 01 00   5 4 3 2 1

Conservatories which are a garden in a building and a building in a garden remain one of the truly exciting areas for collaboration between architects and engineers, landscape architects, and horticulturists, and one of the most genuinely demanding design challenges of our time.

—Anthony Walmsley, FASLA

Who loves a garden loves a greenhouse too.

—William Cowper, 1731–1800

CONTENTS

At the beginning of the twenty-first century, after the convulsions of modernism and the confusions of postmodernism, we look back at the formal elegance of nineteenth-century glasshouses with breathless nostalgia. Personally I'm thinking of the Enid A. Haupt Conservatory at the New York Botanical Garden, near to where I live. It is a magnificent, heavenly cathedral of steel and glass that even in a cynical age somehow embodies the sublimity of the English Romantics. It's like having my own Tintern Abbey close at hand—where I too can "connect the landscape with the quiet of the sky."

The Enid A. Haupt Conservatory is one of a dozen such Victorian glasshouses built in this country at the end of the nineteenth and beginning of the twentieth century. Unfortunately, after a hundred years, few remain. And those that do have required a Trojan effort and great expense to repair and restore. All too often, such structures that once sparkled like diamonds have been consigned to the junk heap—an irrevocable closing of a chapter in architectural history.

The glasshouse was imported to this country from England in the latter half of the nineteenth century, although many other European nations, including France and Germany, had long-standing traditions of building conservatories. But it was the English model that appealed to American tastes, specifically those conservatories that were most simple in their style and ornamentation and yet grand in their purpose. Such conservatories as the Palm House at the Royal Botanic Garden at Kew and Joseph Paxton's Crystal Palace in Hyde Park were admired because they gave even the poorest soul access to the wonderment of nature. Conservatories were democratic.

They were also beautiful. As we can glimpse today, through the example of the

OPPOSITE: *The original Crystal Palace, from the Great Exhibition of 1850–51 in London, impressed visitors with its innovative sense of light and space.*

few left standing, the Victorian conservatory seemed to float or hover. In a way, the conservatory is a type of antiarchitecture. Where most structures in the mid-nineteenth century were crafted of stone and reminded one always of their absolute solidity, these airy structures defied that notion. At times they blended into the sky, at others they shimmered with an uncommon animation. Beyond this, there was a certain subversion of norms. The glasshouse was transparent, allowing views of its superstructure, which hitherto had always been artfully concealed. But in this case, the trusses and beams were revealed and made a prominent component of the aesthetic. A century before the Georges Pompidou center, conservatories in Europe were showing audiences how buildings were built.

In addition to inspiring awe, the great conservatories of the nineteenth century were feats of modern engineering. Conservatory architects were the first designers to use steel, which in the mid-nineteenth century was considered a material only suitable for building bridges. And yet while their colleagues were still plodding along in stone, conservatory architects were experimenting with iron and shaped glass, with the result that their structures soared like skyscrapers. In fact, if you were to trace the history of modern architecture, you would inevitably make your way back to the early conservatories.

Today, conservatories are still architectural laboratories. Innovations in glazing and structural materials continue. Many conservatories of the last few years have pushed the envelope of form, enabled as much by materials as by computer-aided design, with the result that most contemporary glasshouses strike outlandish poses: cylindrical, conoidal, and geodesic, an innovation of the 1960s that already looks dated.

Perhaps the greatest experiment taking place in today's conservatories has to do with finding economical and environmentally sound means for climate control. This has always been a battle, in glasshouses as much as in other architectures. In the 1970s a movement in green architecture got underway that, among other things, sought to develop design strategies that would reduce the dependence upon air-conditioning and heating—two counts on which modern architecture has a disastrous record. Unfortunately, within the

OPPOSITE: *The Rio Grande Botanic Garden Conservatory in Albuquerque, New Mexico.*

larger narrative, green architecture has been abandoned as a fad, to the effect that today we ritually applaud the most wasteful buildings as the best buildings. Conservatories, on the other hand, have never abandoned the green agenda. In terms of hard technology, conservatory design in recent years has driven the development of new, more efficient cooling systems that recycle energy and materials. On the softer side, modern conservatories have also witnessed the maturation of a whole host of design techniques that simply make buildings more efficient, such innovations as passive heating and passive cooling. Still, after more than a hundred years, conservatories provide architects with an important laboratory for thought.

This experimental nature even pervades the landscape architecture of conservatories where, over the last thirty years, revolutionary things have been taking place. Although many conservatories still adhere to the classic Victorian horticultural principles, many others—both new and old—have embraced a new botany, with an emphasis on ecological associations and plant conservation. These are the cutting-edge topics of landscape architecture, and in many ways they are being

most adequately tested in the conservatory. Take a look at places like the Sibley Horticultural Center at Callaway Gardens in Georgia or the new Rio Grande Botanic Garden Conservatory in New Mexico. Radical, but subtle, changes are taking place here— changes that will one day alter the face of the American landscape.

These important laboratories for thought and innovation are spread across America like nodes of enlightenment. What follows is more than an adequate road map. Anne Cunningham has done a marvelous job of bringing together the most important conservatories in the United States into a single tome and, by her astute introduction, given us a lens through which to view them.

Hers is a whirlwind tour that takes us from 1878 to 1996, and from Seattle to Miami. Because Ms. Cunningham chose to organize the material chronologically, we are provided with the rare chance to see how the forms and philosophies of conservatory design have evolved over the years. In her introduction, Ms. Cunningham lays this out for us in explicit terms. But in many ways the more powerful reading is in the text itself, where one can experience a hundred and twenty years in an instant—real time, as it were.

Among the various ideas that emerge, one particular theme dominates. And it is worth noting. At the turn of the century, and up to the Depression, conservatories were seen as a part of the civic repertoire of libraries, ballfields, and parks. And on a typical Sunday afternoon one would have to fight the crowds at the Brooklyn Botanic Garden as much as those at Coney Island. Then, during and after the Second World War, interest in conservatories faded. There was a slight resurgence in the 1960s, but it was nothing like the 1990s. Look to any conservatory today and you will see floods of people: families, couples, and individuals, all of whom are seeking solace, contact with nature, or enlightenment. As Cunningham tells us, modern conservatories have not just sat back and enjoyed the boom. They've reacted and taken the opportunity of market share in order to make a difference. Today, you find

most every conservatory has a public education mission. In addition to redesigning their displays in order to educate, many also run classes and seminars for the public.

There may be many reasons for this. Gardens in general are popular now. But also, it may be that audiences are more sophisticated. People want to learn not just about the newest varieties of *rosa*, but about bigger ideas, such as how natural systems operate or how ecosystems are interconnected. A strong environmental ethic has pervaded the American psyche, and it would not be a stretch to say that, regardless of political affiliation, most people want to see nature preserved. The conservatory is a centerpiece of this movement. It is here, beneath the glorious, sparkling dome that one learns his or her first lessons about the natural world.

These are fundamental lessons, now enabled by a most graceful book. Enter, either vicariously or by getting off the couch, the world of the American conservatory and be amazed. There's still so much to see.

CRYSTAL PALACES

Overview

Garden conservatories across the United States present a glittering, multifaceted landscape. Some of the structures are beautiful vestiges of Victorian art, risen like sparkling phoenixes from the ashes of decay and neglect, and others are hovering in the midst of meticulous and loving restoration. Others are modernist configurations, born during times of optimism and speculation. Still others are contemporary technological wonders with daring architecture and intricate computer-controlled environments. Most of them provide an oasis of color, beauty, and warmth for snow-weary Northerners stranded in long gray winters. All of them celebrate a reverence for plants, while they respond to environmental demands and articulate the need to preserve botanical diversity.

History

The first greenhouses were built in ancient Rome using thin sheets of semitransparent mica rock as glazing. Like traditional cold frames, the squat structures sunk into the earth to protect fragile plants, early greenhouses served utilitarian purposes, such as overwintering fruiting plants. In the eighteenth and nineteenth centuries, with the development of modern glassmaking and the production of structural metals, personal conservatories, greenhouses, stove houses, and orangeries sprung up around Europe. Not surprisingly, these early structures were built by royalty and the aristocratic classes. Although still used for protecting less hardy plants during the winter, gradually conservatories became a focal point of the garden itself, evolving into architectural statements of beauty. In the nineteenth century the mass production of iron and steel

OPPOSITE: *Giant waterplatters at Longwood, given the genus name* Victoria *after England's queen, were the horticultural rage by 1880. They have huge prickly spines underneath, natural notches for rainwater drainage, and ribs strong enough to support the weight of a child.*

accelerated the architectural possibilities, giving rise to larger and more expansive conservatories. At the same time municipalities and large cities started building grand public conservatories, in part as community entertainment, and in part as a badge of worth to show to the world. France, Germany, and England all saw enormous glasshouses erected in their cities as a result of World's Fairs or other large exhibitions.

Two British conservatories, in particular, caught the imagination of designers worldwide. Richard Turner and Decimus Burton finished the Palm House at the Royal Botanic Gardens at Kew, on the outskirts of London, in 1848, and it quickly became one of the most popular institutions in England. Only a few years later, landscape gardener Joseph Paxton stunned the world with his competition-winning design for the immense Crystal Palace, part of London's Great Exhibition of 1851. The Crystal Palace covered eighteen acres in Hyde Park, enclosing even the majestic old elm trees. At 1,800 linear feet, the sheer size of the structure became a spectacularly beautiful symbol of British world dominance. Using a rational system of iron framing, Paxton created a vaulted 108-foot

span, as tall as Notre Dame Cathedral in Paris. The entire structure was covered with nearly a million square feet of sheet glass, estimated to be about a third of the country's annual glass production. But its lasting effect was far more pragmatic. In order to finish the building under a tight six-month deadline, Paxton developed a modular system so that much of the structure was prefabricated off-site and then assembled in the park all at once. Afterward it was effectively dismantled in sections and rebuilt on an estate outside of the city.

As early as the eighteenth century, a few wealthy landowners and horticulturists in America experimented with small glasshouses. George Washington's estate at Mount Vernon boasted a greenhouse, as did the Philadelphia garden of his friend, plant explorer John Bartram. But it was not until 1880 that the American aristocracy got their first view of the European luxury in the form of industrialist Jay Gould's immense glasshouse at Lyndhurst, his estate in New York's Hudson River Valley. To design the structure, Gould hired Frederick A. Lord and William Burnham, whose fledgling firm had built several greenhouses in upstate New

York. But this structure was far more ambitious than anything the firm had attempted previously, requiring a curvilinear steel frame. The success of their first commission brought Lord & Burnham a host of new clients in both the private and public sector.

While other wealthy Americans continued emulating European gentry by building private conservatories on their estates well into the twentieth century, the architectural form of glasshouses was most fully developed in the city parks. Enamored by the democratic spirit of the Palm House at Kew and the logic of Paxton's Crystal Palace, American cities followed suit in the last decades of the nineteenth century with a series of glass-enclosed public gardens. In 1853, on the heels of Paxton's triumph in London, a similarly prefabricated structure was constructed at the New York's World's Fair. In 1876, Philadelphia set a new standard with its splendid Horticultural Hall, built for the country's Centennial Exhibition. Unfortunately both of these remarkable structures were destroyed by fire.

But this did not quench the desire for creating places within the urban fabric where people could gather in a natural setting. The latter half of the nineteenth century was the

era of the City Beautiful movement, during which great civic parks were created in burgeoning cities. Frederick Law Olmsted and Calvert Vaux designed New York's Central Park in 1857, and their influence spread across dozens of similar parks over the next fifty years. Conservatories were an important part of these landscapes. San Francisco was a leader with the 1878 Lick Conservatory in Golden Gate Park, and major city parks from coast to coast scrambled to catch up. Lord & Burnham designed Phipps Conservatory in Pittsburgh, and when it opened in 1893 it was briefly the largest in the United States. New York's Central Park had a flower conservatory from 1899 to 1934.

Lord & Burnham modeled Lyndhurst, the first steel-frame conservatory in the United States, after the Royal Botanic Garden glasshouse at Kew.

The great era of Victorian glasshouses in the United States ended in the 1930s with the Depression, and when the country finally emerged after the wars, the gusto for these kinds of public works had exhausted itself. The middle decades of the twentieth century were a dark period for public conservatories, inspiring no new innovations and lots of bad renovations. Delicate glass entryways were replaced by mismatched concrete fronts. Decorative iron scrollwork was removed entirely, in some cases leaving an impression of nothing more than a barn-like greenhouse. In some conservatories metal guy wires were installed to hold up weakened cupolas, but they had the effect of suggesting laundry lines and attracted pigeons. In the worst cases, underused portions of historic structures were simply chopped off, leaving lopsided architecture and central domes that were no longer in the center.

During the 1960s, partly impelled by the emergence of environmentalism, conservatory building rallied. The most significant architectural influence was R. Buckminster Fuller's geodesic dome, of which the Climatron® at the Missouri Botanical Garden is the best known. Fuller designed with nature, creating his structures so that they were easy and efficient to heat and cool. They also appealed to the space-age aesthetic soon to overtake tastes in everything from clothing design to visual art. By the middle of the decade, engineers and architects tinkered with Fuller's original idea, expanding and adjusting the form to create new technology for controlling the climate within. Milwaukee's distinctive Mitchell Park Domes and Denver's Boettcher Memorial Conservatory, both fabricated from concrete, stand out among experimental conservatories that expanded the geodesic dome to new shapes.

A combination of ingenuity and computers nudged conservatories even further away from the traditional Victorian scheme of an E-shaped building with a dome in the center. In 1984 Oklahoma City built the Crystal Bridge, a clear cylindrical tube that spans a shallow lake in the city's botanical garden. The aluminum and stainless steel pyramids of The Lucille Halsell Conservatory in San Antonio and the Rio Grande Botanic Garden in Albuquerque are excellent examples of how computer-aided design and revolutionary building materials enable architects to rethink the way glasshouses are built.

Structure

Garden conservatories are some of the most difficult public buildings to design and maintain. Architectural creativity and horticultural needs vie with public comfort and safety and require compromise to meet myriad government regulations. The misty level of 90 percent humidity that benefits tropical plants simultaneously wilts people and wreaks havoc on structural materials and paint. Mosses that enhance rock formations become a public safety hazard when they migrate across stone and brick walkways. Construction codes and requirements of the Americans with Disabilities Act present challenges to landscape architects trying to recreate a natural jungle; yet clever solutions abound, as in Denver's Boettcher Memorial Conservatory where a huge concrete banyan tree has stairs hidden inside, along with an elevator to lift wheelchairs above the high foliage for optimum viewing.

The structural history of conservatories parallels the history of building technologies—specifically, how metal and glass have evolved over the years. In the nineteenth century, rapid developments in each of these fields enabled architects to create fantastic

OPPOSITE
TOP: *Missouri Botanical Garden's Climatron® was the first of several glasshouses that took inspiration from R. Buckminster Fuller.*
BOTTOM: *Denver's Boettcher Memorial Conservatory found a creative solution to accessibility by building an elevator inside a concrete replica of a banyan tree.*

vaulted domes clad in a translucent skin. Iron was the backbone that made it happen, providing a much-needed alternative to wood, which was not only easily incinerated by untended boilers but also subject to rot and decay. Metal also appeared as an artistic statement and was scrolled, rolled, and hammered into ornamentation, in some instances creating an almost rococo covering of the exterior surface. By the 1880s, iron was the building material of choice for new conservatories in the United States, although a few holdouts continued to use wood, including the Como Park Conservatory in St. Paul, Minnesota, which specified as late as 1914 the use of "clear air-dried California redwood or Louisiana Red cypress."

As years passed, glasshouse manufacturers watched their iron and structural steel conservatories deteriorate from the same high humidity, corrosive fertilizers, and leaks in the glazing systems that destroyed wooden frames. After the Jazz Age, aluminum looked like a promising alternative, and in 1932 the *Engineering News-Record* praised the new United States Botanic Garden in Washington, D.C., for being the first building to use aluminum as a structural material. Their Lord & Burn-

ham design took advantage of the new metal's added strength to create artfully cantilevered roof trusses for the dome. A little more than a decade later, improved technology extended to popular greenhouses, and Lord & Burnham announced with pride that they had a "method of eliminating outside painting and maintenance costs through use of aluminum glazing strips known as Barcaps." But early aluminum had trouble dealing with the climate, becoming discolored and pockmarked. In the later decades more versatile steel alloys came to the fore, better able to withstand the ravages of time, though various forms of aluminum are still used.

Ever since the Romans experimented with mica, glass has been the bane of conservatories. Although wooden and metal structures inevitably suffer from high humidity and other climatic hazards, notoriously it has been the glazing, or architectural glass, that has been the most difficult element to maintain in a glasshouse. Blowing glass was a laborious process with inevitable imperfections such as unevenness. In the eighteenth century a technique for pouring molten glass and then rolling it was developed, but it was not until the mid-nineteenth century, when glasshouse production reached a much larger scale, that the technique was standardized. As new metals enabled the architectural form of conservatories to become more visually interesting and more graceful, glassmakers were presented with the challenge of making curved glass. Developments in the poured methods such as cooled molds made curved glass possible but costly, because every time a pane in a glasshouse broke it had to be custom-ordered. For a brief time in the United States, overlapping flat panes seemed like a solution. The Garfield Park Conservatory in Chicago, built in 1907, tried lapped glass, but condensation built up between the overlapping edges then froze and expanded. Frigid winter days echoed with a symphony of breaking glass, and the country's largest conservatory had to replace all the glazing after a few years.

Few conservatories can boast that they possess their original glazing, in part because disasters, both natural and man-made, are too common. When stockpiled dynamite exploded in a nearby wooded area, all the glass on the eastern side of the conservatory in the New York Botanical Garden shattered. A fierce windstorm caused tremendous dam-age to Phipps Conservatory in 1937, hailstones destroyed much of Como Park's building in 1962, and Hurricane Andrew demolished Fairchild's Rare Plant House in Miami in 1992. Excessively heavy snows have crushed segments of many conservatories in the North, taking a huge toll on the tender plant stock within. Early solutions for falling glass included installing netting just below the roof level and embedding wire into the glass during construction as was done in the original dome of the United States Botanic Garden in Washington, D.C. Just like the structural members, glazing is subject to the vagaries of sun, water, and fertilizers, all of which weaken the glass, reduce its translucence, and disintegrate the adhesives used to secure it in place.

In the 1960s plastic emerged as an alternative to glass. But it quickly proved inadequate as it yellowed under hot sun and corroded from contact with chemical fertilizers and joint adhesives. Not only was the yellowing unsightly, but the plants suffered from lack of light. In 1960, St. Louis' innovative Climatron® conservatory installed thick, wide panes of Plexiglas for better insulation and a clearer visual expanse between

The conservatory in San Francisco not only suffered from broken glass but also lost a significant number of plants when they were destroyed by glass shards and low temperatures.

supports. But within twenty years it had to be replaced with a new acrylic glass. When traditional glazing was determined unfeasible for the new Crystal Bridge in Oklahoma City in 1984, a double-walled, translucent material called Exolite™ was developed in order to completely wrap the cylindrical construction. In recent years, driven in part by a dissatisfaction with plastic alternatives, conservatories have returned to using glass. In some cases architects have constrained themselves to linear forms in order to do so. The partially sunken Lucille Halsell Conservatory in San Antonio, designed as a series of pyramids above ground, successfully used laminated, heat-strengthened glass that is only 9/16" thick with a smooth appearance. Another underground building, the Steinhardt Conservatory in Brooklyn, used a combination of double-glazed laminated glass overhead for the roof portions and single-glazed annealed glass for the vertical walls that rise above ground level.

Exhibits

The landscape architecture of conservatories has evolved hand-in-hand with the architecture, inspired by changes in taste and culture, as well as the development of new technologies and attitudes toward nature.

Early exhibits were typically very formal, mimicking the gardens of the Renaissance, with geometric beds and architectural ornamentation such as gates, benches and statuary to provide focal points for the eye. The horticultural approach was Linnean, with pottted plants arranged according to families and species, as described by the eighteenth-century botanist Carolus Linnæus. The scientific and rationalist approach accommodated the artful, and the Victorian glasshouse was considered a place where nature was perfected.

But in the early twentieth century, Chicago landscape architect Jens Jensen changed glasshouse displays forever when he installed the plant collections at Garfield Park Conservatory. Jensen's scheme was intentionally naturalistic, with jagged stonework, babbling brooks, and plants mixed together in a layered tapestry that resembled a real forest or jungle. He hid heating pipes behind rock walls. Throughout the twentieth century, naturalistic landscaping has provided a foil against which the Victorian ideals of order and artifice have been

cast. The display philosophy of today's conservatories covers the full spectrum. Pennsylvania's Longwood Gardens continues founder Pierre Du Pont's unabashed imitation of the great show gardens of Europe, while at Sibley Horticultural Center in Georgia, the subtle philosophy of Jensen is the guiding force.

In the last decades of the twentieth century a new emphasis on imitating actual ecosystems took hold at many conservatories, where plants are arranged according to climatic zone and interdependent associations. Like Jensen's displays, the ecosystem idea is to create a naturalistic setting. But hard science is brought into the equation, in order to create a truthful telling of how nature really operates. One example of this trend is the recently refurbished Enid A. Haupt Conservatory at The New York Botanical Garden. The classic Victorian structure was restored faithfully to its 1900 original, while inside a revolution took place, where traditional glasshouse fare was replaced with a more flowing organization, much like an ecosystem itself.

As part of this new approach to design, many conservatories take a proactive stance

San Antonio's Lucille Halsell Conservatory plant collection resides below ground level while the visionary glass pyramids rise up to let in the brilliant Texas light all year round.

Colorful poison dart frogs at the Missouri Botanical Garden add another dimension to the tropical theme.

toward educating their audiences about the environment. In most modern glasshouses visitors see displays of rare and endangered plants accompanied by information about plant conservation. A few conservatories take the "think globally, act locally" approach by highlighting plants from the local region, as opposed to showing species from some far away rainforest. The increasingly critical need for water management is also a universal topic. Particularly in warmer climates, conservatories showcase ways to use native plants, rather than exotics, in order to save water and reduce the need for pesticides.

Animals have been an integral part of conservatories since the nineteenth century. Sometimes these guests wandered in unintentionally, as in 1916, when a ring-tailed cat escaped from the Bronx Zoo and took refuge in a tall palm tree under the dome of The New York Botanical Garden's conservatory. But more commonly, animals were used to enhance the display. Alligators in shallow pools were part of the exotic atmosphere in the early days at both the Phipps Conservatory and Lyndhurst. Today the fauna tends to be less threatening, though the Atlanta Botanical Garden Conservatory does feature

an aquarium of poison dart frogs and the Missouri Botanical Garden is building an arachnid cage for its Desert House.

Parrots and tropical birds fly freely through a number of conservatories, while other glasshouses keep birds in cages to contain droppings and plant damage. Butterflies have become so popular that whole conservatories have been built just for them, most notably the Cecil B. Day Butterfly Conservatory at Georgia's Callaway Gardens. In an effort to lure families and entertain children, many garden conservatories have butterfly shows as part of their summer programs. A few organizations encourage butterflies to inhabit their regular displays, ignoring the conflict between caterpillars that can damage plants and the popular butterflies they become. The major drawback of free-flying butterflies and birds is the need for extra netting on windows and vents, double doors, and higher and more consistent levels of heat than most conservatories choose to use, particularly at night.

One of the battles that conservatories constantly fight is that against pests and diseases. In the past, gardeners used an armada of toxic chemicals to keep the collection appearing healthy; however, in recent years conservatories have turned toward more enlightened methods, such as Integrated Pest Management (IPM), which emphasizes improved cultural practices, the continued visual monitoring of the collection and the identification of which insects are good and which are bad. The latter are picked off plants, or in some cases the former are enlisted to help in their eradication. IPM also encourages amphibians and other small animals that prey on pests. As a result of using fewer toxic chemicals, today's conservatories are generally healthier places with a whole assortment of small insect-eating creatures like frogs, toads, turtles, and lizards that help reduce the number of damaging insects.

Infrastructure

What visitors do not see has been as important as what they do see throughout the history of conservatories. Behind the displays are catacombs of heating and cooling machines, as well as offices, classrooms and research facilities. As in a museum or zoo, the interior design of conservatories strives to conceal the inner workings of the institu-

tion and keep visitors' attention focused on plants. Nonetheless, dealing with the caprices of the elements and cultural requirements of different plants has required the development of complex building technologies.

Heating vast amounts of space with only glass as an insulator is an uphill battle. Until 1816, glasshouses relied upon passive solar heat, decomposing fertilizer in the soil, or unreliable steam heat. Hot-water heating then became popular, but it required huge amounts of fuel and had very little direct heating surface. Lord & Burnham put their first boiler on the market in 1873 and refined the immense contraptions over the next few decades. The overall heating was more uniform, but stoking the fires for the largest conservatories required constant manpower at the boilers, often three shifts in a twenty-four-hour period, every single day of the year.

Modern conservatories rely, at least partially, upon sophisticated automatic controls to regulate atmosphere, air flow and temperature. A popular misting device, the Mee Fog System, adds spectral mist while helping tropical plants thrive. Computer-regulated

Exhibits of threatened tropical species such as Theobroma cacao *become more meaningful when visitors realize that someday the source of chocolate may be extinct.*

ABOVE: *The conservatory at Long-wood Gardens covered nearly four acres in 1926, and it was heated by these four boilers tended twenty-four hours a day.*
OPPOSITE: *The Orangery at Long-wood Gardens, c. 1930, where vents along the walkways conducted warmth from an underground maze of heating pipes.*

orchid cases give rare specimens ideal grow-ing conditions while they protect them from theft. At the apex of constantly monitored atmosphere, Lucille Halsell Conservatory's central computer communicates with two sensors located in each room every sixty sec-onds, taking temperature and humidity readings then sending the average back to the central computer. Simultaneously, an out-side weather station checks wind speed and direction, rainfall, and light intensity. The computer then coordinates the sensor read-ings and sets into motion whatever action is necessary to reach the programmed targets—a

far cry from the old days of drafty hand-cranked vents.

Thanks to meticulously plotted glass angles and carefully situated buildings, con-servatories in Texas and New Mexico rely on a fair amount of solar energy to supply heat in their mild climates. The Sibley Horticul-tural Center in Georgia is so well situated, it requires no summer cooling, though the glazing in many other glass houses makes summer temperatures unbearable. Most conservatories find that evaporative cooling cells, combined with high-powered fans, attain a comfortable medium between the needs of plants and those of the visitors. Air-conditioning is usually installed only in lob-bies, restaurants, and gift shops.

Behind the scenes, support and produc-tion houses are just as important as the part of the conservatory seen by the public. In addition to artistic designers, talented gar-deners bring plants to perfection in auxiliary greenhouses before they go on display. Some exhibits, such as orchids, rotate almost daily so that visitors see only plants in bloom. Sea-sonal exhibits, in which flowers and plants change on a specific schedule, require intri-cate timing and overproduction to be sure the public sees only the best. The standard ratio is about three support houses for each conservatory. And every institution, even those that maintain naturalistic landscapes with little daily change, is indebted to the knowledgeable horticulturists who keep the displays alive and thriving.

Another infrastructure issue for modern conservatories is water. Many sections of the country have suffered from drought at one time or another, and few industries feel the impact as much as those growing plants. Occasional city regulations for conservatories already call for collection and reuse of runoff water that flows down drains under normal watering conditions. More aggressive solutions must be found, and Como Park's conservatory in St. Paul seems to have one of the best. At the time of their 1998 renovation, they designed special gutters into the structure to collect as much as twelve thousand gallons of rainwater in underground cisterns, then pump it back for use in the conservatory.

Even though computers can operate complex watering systems, conservatories of all sizes prefer to water some displays by hand in order to give each plant the precise amount of moisture it needs under variable daily

conditions. With too little water, plant growth is stunted or it dies; too much water and the plants drown or rot. Glasshouses require an uninterrupted flow of good water to maintain the high quality of their exhibits. City water supplies often carry more chemicals than many plants—particularly those gathered from the wild—can tolerate. In addition to collecting rainwater, conservatories look for other ways to avoid chemically treated water, such as ionization or the reverse-osmosis system used in the Bolz Conservatory in Madison, Wisconsin.

The Future

The Victorian public embraced conservatories because they believed in the restorative powers of strolling in the park and communing with nature. They were also fascinated, aesthetically and scientifically, by exotic flora. Plant lovers in the twenty-first century echo similar sentiments, but with a number of differences. For instance, today we have a much better understanding of ecology and how ecosystems operate. This has given rise to an understanding of the implications of endangered species and the need for global protection. Validating their existence even more, glasshouses across the country are official rescue sites for endangered plants seized by government agencies intercepting them from smugglers.

Conservatories convey their messages—whether environmental, artistic, or educational—in various ways and at different levels: signs and interpretive storyboards accompany plant displays, docents and recorded guides offer more detailed insight into the significance of plants and their place in our lives, and expert horticulturists conduct myriad classes throughout the year. Just about every conservatory gives school tours and provides interactive learning opportunities for children. Garfield Park and Longwood have outstanding indoor children's gardens, while others offer fine outdoor summer camps and gardening programs for youngsters. Florida's Fairchild Tropical Garden deserves high praise for having signs and brochures in both English and Spanish. In sum, today's modern conservatory has become a locus for understanding and caretaking of the natural world.

Renewed public interest and support for conservatories around the country proves that this approach to exhibits, both formal and informal, is successful. Whether the glasshouses are high-tech wonder-constructions or modest remodels of old neighborhood favorites, they continue to collect and display plants with a sense of urgency. The *New York Times* summed it up on May 1, 1997, when describing the opening of the Enid A. Haupt Conservatory: "in the years separating us from the Victorians, our relationship to nature has profoundly changed. What we seek to conserve now is not individual plants, transplanted from their native habitats, but rather nature itself."

Conservatory of Flowers

GOLDEN GATE PARK, SAN FRANCISCO, CALIFORNIA

Although steel was readily available as a building material by the 1870s, San Francisco's conservatory was constructed entirely of wood, from the load-bearing, structural elements to the exterior decorative scrollwork. The stories of its origin have grown large over the years, with some claiming that the material was purchased from an English manufacturer and shipped to San Francisco, but local experts insist the redwood was harvested and milled in California. No records exist to prove or disprove either assertion.

People do agree, however, that land speculator and piano maker James Lick (1796–1876) ordered the prefabricated redwood sections to build a personal conservatory on his estate in the Santa Clara Valley but died before he could construct it. After his death, a group of prominent Californians bought the unassembled kit from his estate and gave it to the city in order to erect a public conservatory in Golden Gate Park.

The city hired Frederick A. Lord, of Lord's Horticultural Manufacturing Co. in Irvington, New York (later to become Lord & Burnham), to construct the building, and by the time it opened in the summer of 1878, the Lick Conservatory attracted visitors by the thousands to the newly developed Golden Gate Park. Only a dozen years earlier, landscape architect Frederick Law Olmsted told the city fathers not to bother creating a park in San Francisco, because the lack of tall

OPPOSITE: *Plastic sheets cover gaping holes where glass was blown out in the devastating 1995 storm that closed the conservatory.*

*Even in foggy San Francisco,
glasshouses use whitewash to help
shade delicate plants inside against
bright summer sun.*

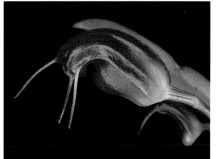

LEFT: Zamia lindenii, *a rare stiff-leaved cycad with a gigantic cone-like flower cluster, is one of five permanent plants that will remain in place during renovation.*

TOP RIGHT: Masdevallia limax, *part of the conservatory's famous collection of five thousand orchids.*

BOTTOM RIGHT: *The orchid* Masdevallia decumana.

*Colored glass window vents around
the building add variety to the tints of
plants and flowers as the sunlight
shifts during the day.*

trees there meant that it could never be as beautiful as New York or London.

A stunning, spectral landmark in the park, the conservatory has had its share of disasters. In 1883, a boiler fire raged out of control and destroyed the main dome. When it was rebuilt in 1890, it was redesigned in a much more ornate Victorian style with elaborate redwood scrollwork and colorful glass panels. Miraculously that new conservatory survived the earthquake of 1906, another fire in 1918, and limped through a devastating windstorm in 1995 that shattered more than 30,000 panes of glass and destroyed over 15 percent of the plants.

Golden Gate Park's conservatory is the oldest wooden glasshouse in the United States, but time and the inevitable combination of water and harsh chemicals have damaged most of the wooden frame and ornamentation. A major renovation is underway to modernize the infrastructure, reconstitute the plant collection, and deal with the inevitable rot afflicting the wood.

Because the conservatory is listed as an historic structure, the architects are taking great care to adhere to the 1890 design as much as possible. As they dismantle the building, they plan to reuse any original wood in good condition. The configuration of the original glasshouse led some experts to believe the early construction was based upon shipbuilding principals. No nails were used; only pine pitch holds the unusual S-shaped joints together. And if the building framework is viewed with imagination, picturing it upside down, the curve of the roofline looks exactly like a ship's hull.

The conservatory's plant collection, highlighted by thousands of high altitude cool-growing orchids, hundreds of bromeliads, carnivores and cycads, will be protected and moved around ahead of the wrecking ball. Five of their largest and most valuable specimens, most notably a one hundred year old towering philodendron and a very rare cycad, *Zamia lindenii,* will remain in place with protective shields built around them for the period of restoration.

YEAR OPENED
1878

HEIGHT
67 feet

AREA
12,000 square feet

CONSERVATORY HOURS
closed for renovation
until 2003

LOCATION
John F. Kennedy Drive
Golden Gate Park
San Francisco, CA 94117

FURTHER INFORMATION
(415) 666-7017
www.frp.org

Conservatories at the
Missouri Botanical Garden

*T*he Missouri Botanical Garden has always been at the forefront of horticulture in America. Conceived by intrepid businessman Henry Shaw in an effort to preserve the prairie, long before ecology and native plants were in vogue, the garden has grown over the last 150 years into an enormous public garden and renowned research facility. The garden complex showcases three conservatory structures, with a new one on the way.

The oldest building is the Linnean House built in 1882 and named for Carl Linnæaus (1707–1778) who originated the system of plant classification. Originally designed by George I. Barnett in brick with large, south-facing windows, the building was used by Shaw to overwinter large potted palms, ferns, and citrus trees that moved outdoors in the late spring. The small conservatory is still in use, making it the oldest continually operating glasshouse west of the Mississippi; however, its character has evolved. At the end of World War I, the roof was removed and constructed in glass, and permanent beds were installed around a small, naturalistic water feature. After a hailstorm in 1927 the roof was converted to partial slate and the planting design altered to showcase camellias that thrive in a cool environment. Today, during the winter months, this venerable collection provides a dazzling show, the centerpiece of which is the rare yellow *Camellia chrysantha*, coveted for hybridizing.

OPPOSITE: *Built in 1882, the Linnean House is the oldest continually operating display greenhouse in the United States.*

TOP: *The geodesic dome of the Climatron® inspired myriad variations in conservatories for decades to come.* MIDDLE: *A recreated Moorish garden and an antique portico help display the Shoenberg's temperate flora.* BOTTOM: *Camellias and cyclamen thrive in the cool temperatures of the Linnean House.*

In contrast to the *ancien* spirit of the Linnean House, the Climatron® presents us with a vision of the future, even though it is now forty years old. The geodesic design was based upon the writings and drawings of futurist R. Buckminster Fuller. Although today there are many geodesic dome-like conservatories around the United States, this was the first actually to be built. Originally, Plexiglas hung on the external aluminum tubing structure, but it crazed, became clouded, and was replaced between 1988 and 1990 with a superior heat-strengthened Saflex laminated glass.

Inside the dome the planting design presents a lush tropical rainforest where plants are allowed to grow as they would in the jungle. This is not a visibly manicured garden, but rather a haven in which rare and endangered species have a chance to thrive: More than half the species were collected from the wild. The walking path creates an immersion experience. Visitors walk under waterfalls, over bridges, and through the middle of display areas that showcase plants with industrial and economic uses or other areas where rainforest ecology is explained. Two favorite attractions are the river aquarium tank built into one of the naturalistic fiberglass rock formations and filled with Amazonian fish, and the delicate

The striking Shoenberg Temperate House, on one side of the Climatron®, is offset by its mirror-image Desert House on the other side.

RIGHT: *Free-flying butterflies provide a kaleidoscope of changing contrasts as they land on flowers and plants, such as this bromeliad,* Billbergia euthemiae rubra. BELOW: *Waterfalls are a major part of the tropical rain forest display in the Climatron®.*

butterflies and small free-flying tropical birds that flit through the air and add to the exotic atmosphere.

The garden's preeminent horticulturists and experts in botanical research carefully selected more than 3,500 tropical plants for the Climatron® with an eye toward mimicking the biodiversity of the world's rainforests. Underlying their efforts is the theory that the more people become knowledgeable about these unique ecosystems, the more they are apt to work toward saving them. Expanding on this idea, educational displays in the adjoining Brookings Interpretive Center reinforce the significance of tropical rainforest destruction and delineate the vital role of plants in our planet's ecosystems. Within the conservatory the incredible array of unusual plants includes the largest indoor Screw Pine (*Pandanus copelandii*) native to the Philippines, a rare double-coconut palm, and myriad exotic gingers. The cycads, many of which were saved from the World's Fair held in St. Louis in 1904, include a rare epiphytic species.

The Shoenberg Temperate House was built in 1990. Interior temperatures are a little cooler than in the Climatron® and the plant palette focuses on Mediterranean themes such as figs, olives, cork, and an assortment of riparian plants that thrive along riverbanks in semiarid climates. Other display areas include a biblical garden and a bog teeming with carnivorous plants. The highlight of the conservatory is a colorful walled garden with a fountain and tilework based upon the eleventh-century Moorish garden at the Alhambra in Granada, Spain. Interpretive signs review the history of formal garden design.

On the boards is a new Desert House, scheduled to open in 2003. It is a structural mirror image of the Shoenberg Temperate House, but the glass slopes away from the central Climatron® dome. North American desert plants fill one half of the house; the remaining half is split between plants from South African deserts and the endangered spiny thorn forest of Madagascar, where the Missouri Botanical Garden has an active research and conservation program. The split level house has entrances at both levels and an elevator hidden in the artificial rockwork. In addition to the open Sonoran reptile pit, a number of small animal and arachnid cages lurk in the rockwork.

YEAR OPENED
1878

HEIGHT
Linnean House: 22 feet
Climatron®: 70 feet
Shoenberg Temperate House: 40 feet
Desert House:. 40 feet

AREA
Linnean House: 4,290 square feet
Climatron®: 24,000 square feet
Shoenberg Temperate House: 8,900 square feet
Desert House: 8,900 square feet

CONSERVATORY HOURS
Daily 9:00 a.m. to 5:00 p.m., Wednesday and Saturday 7:00 a.m. to 5:00 p.m.; Open until 8:00 p.m. Memorial Day through Labor Day

LOCATION
4344 Shaw Boulevard
St. Louis, MO 63110

FURTHER INFORMATION
(314) 577-9400
or (800) 642-8842
www.mobot.org

Lincoln Park Conservatory
& Garfield Park Conservatory

LINCOLN PARK, CHICAGO, ILLINOIS; GARFIELD PARK, CHICAGO, ILLINOIS

*A*t the turn of the century, bolstered by international attention brought by the great World's Columbian Exposition of 1893, Chicago was booming. As has always been the case in the development of cities, the flourishing middle class clamored for amusements and entertainment such as beaches, baseball fields, libraries, and gardens. The city parks department and powerful garden club took the lead, developing a series of public landscapes that in some respects remain unrivaled.

A key ingredient to park building in the Chicago climate was the establishment of the city's two conservatories, hailed by critics at the turn of the century as innovative works of art, both in terms of architecture and land-scape design. Today, though still important structures, each reflects the changes in the neighborhoods that surround it. Lincoln Park, on Chicago's lakefront, north of the Loop, receives thousands of visitors per year. Garfield Park Conservatory, located within Garfield Park on the west side of town, sadly sees only about one tenth as many people.

Located next to a popular zoo, the Lincoln Park Conservatory reminds visitors of the peripatetic spirit of the Victorians. Architect Joseph L. Silsbee designed the bell-shaped, hipped roof upon a Saracenic theme, suggesting that the plants within were from faraway places like Arabia. Silsbee used copper glazing bars in addition to the iron beams and roof trusses to imbue the building

OPPOSITE: *Shortly after the assassination of President Lincoln, Lake Park and its conservatory were renamed in his honor. This photo dates from the 1890s.*

with gleaming brilliance. Inside, the plant collections include tropical species from a variety of ecosystems and zones, including prehistoric cycads and a healthy collection of palms. Two magnificent Scheelea Palms (*Scheelea leandroana*), have flourished here for decades, grown from seeds collected during a 1926 expedition.

Descending a small stairway, visitors enter the Fern Room, sunk below ground level to help maintain high humidity and create the ambiance of a misty grotto. In an adjoining room are tropical orchids, bromeliads, and other epiphytes. The orchid collection provides year round bloom with Dendrobiums, Vandas, Cattleyas, and many other species of botanical interest. Continuing their long tradition of flower shows, Lincoln Park's Show House mounts five seasonal exhibitions each year.

Garfield Park Conservatory is one of the largest conservatories in the country. The structure was designed by landscape architect Jens Jensen, in conjunction with Hitchings and Company, with gently rounded rooflines that suggest the mounded haystacks of the Midwest. Inside, Jensen eschewed the usual floral collections and bench displays arranged

OPPOSITE: *Garfield Park Conservatory was put on the National Register of Historic Places by the United States Department of the Interior.*
THIS PAGE:
Lincoln Park (top) aimed for an exotic look in conservatory design. Across town, the roof of the Garfield Park Conservatory (bottom) was inspired by the shape of haystacks in Midwestern fields.

BELOW: *Statuary is an important element in many displays at Garfield.*
BOTTOM: *At Lincoln, the plant collections include tropical species from a variety of ecosystems and zones, including prehistoric cycads and a healthy collection of palms.*

ABOVE: *The tropical displays at Garfield include a double-coconut palm, which boasts the largest seed in the plant kingdom.*

by botanical family. He planted specimens directly into the ground in fluid landscapes with interwoven brick pathways and water features. In the Fern Room, a sunken grotto appended to the main structure, he used stratified stonework that not only hides the heating pipes but also creates realistic settings for the displays, so that the observer becomes immersed in the experience. This naturalistic approach may seem commonplace today, but at the beginning of the twentieth century it was visionary.

The collection originally was full of exotics brought by plant explorers and their wealthy patrons. Of these, many notables have survived to this day, including a double-coconut palm (*Lodoicea maldivica*) that was planted in place from seed, the largest seed in the plant kingdom.

Unfortunately decades of deferred maintenance have seen the huge building suffer. The glass roof of the Palm House was replaced in 1958 with a more economical but ultimately unsightly fiberglass skin, which itself has since been replaced twice. Old steam pipes burst during the bitterly cold winter of 1994, resulting in the devastating loss of 80 percent of the plants in the Aroid House. Finally the city took notice, and today the conservatory is experiencing a rebirth that includes the construction of an outstanding children's garden, one of the country's largest available to kids in winter (most are outdoors). Part garden, part science exhibit, and part playground, the new addition appeals to the curiosity and energy of elementary school children. Although not as crowded and animated as its sister conservatory across town, Garfield Park Conservatory promises a much needed and appreciated revival.

GARFIELD PARK CONSERVATORY

YEAR OPENED
1908

HEIGHT
65 feet

AREA
92,770 square feet

CONSERVATORY HOURS
Daily 9:00 a.m. to 5:00 p.m., including holidays

LOCATION
300 North Central Park Avenue
Chicago, IL 60624

FURTHER INFORMATION
(312) 746-5100
www.garfield-conservatory.org

LINCOLN PARK CONSERVATORY

YEAR OPENED
1890

AREA
20,504 square feet

LOCATION
2400 N. Stockton Drive
Chicago, IL 60614

HEIGHT
50 feet

CONSERVATORY HOURS
Daily 9:00 a.m. to 5:00 p.m., including holidays

FURTHER INFORMATION
(312) 742-7736

Phipps Conservatory

*P*hipps Conservatory is a reminder of Pittsburgh's greatness in the time when Andrew Carnegie and Henry Phipps helped transform the American landscape with steel, steam engines, and civic philanthropy. Among his many contributions, Phipps (1839–1930) gave the city a conservatory "for public instruction and pleasure" in the newly developed Schenley Park. Designed and erected by the New York firm of Lord & Burnham in 1893, the Phipps Conservatory was a shimmering Romanesque-style edifice of steel, cypress, stone, and glass.

But there were no plants. Luckily the World's Columbian Exposition in Chicago closed just two months later, and the entire tropical plant display was shipped by train across the Midwest in time for the debut of the conservatory. Curiously, there was no fanfare; they simply opened the doors one day, and people began to wander in from the park. Instantly popular, the conservatory added three more rooms in 1896, and Lord & Burnham finished the final structure, the Desert Room, in 1902.

Since then, the conservatory has traveled the road from elegance to disrepair—and back. Shortly after it opened, the Palm Court showed off exotic alligators in a tropical pool. By the 1930s, rats and weeds competed for space. A savage storm in 1937 damaged the big glasshouse and destroyed the support greenhouses in the back. By 1940, WPA crews had reconstructed the production

OPPOSITE: *When it was built, Phipps became the largest conservatory in the country.*

Decorating for the fall flower show
goes beyond colorful
chrysanthemums.

Beautiful gardens outside the conser-
vatory add to Phipps's overall appeal.

houses, but the conservatory continued to suffer from natural deterioration and inconsistent community support. A flurry of activity in the late 1970s began the renaissance that continued until 1993 when a private foundation purchased Phipps Conservatory and focused on bringing it back to its original glory. Today the thirteen different rooms resound with elaborate exhibits such as the Parterre de Broderie, the Tropical Fruit and Spice Room, and the Victoria Room, named after the largest water lily in the world, *Victoria regia*. In the Broderie Room visitors stand on an elevated terrace and gaze down upon a formal seventeenth-century French-style knot garden designed with geometric patterning of low boxwood hedges and bright flowers. Additional rooms feature spectacular miniature orchids and displays that showcase the meticulous art of bonsai. The Stove Room comes alive each summer with thirty-one different varieties of butterflies and moths. Instead of importing all the delicate creatures, Phipps's staff raise some on host plants like passion vines.

Outreach, in the form of educational programs and marketing, plays an important role in the conservatory's renewal. Three annual flower shows and other special events centered around holidays are counted upon to bring in crowds as well as add color to the space. In terms of education, the conservatory offers a variety of classes and games for children and informative horticultural lectures for adults.

The enormous structure wraps around itself, with a large transverse axis containing the central palm dome and two parallel axes that extend toward the rear to create an enclosed courtyard. Originally this exterior space was conceived as a diorama to be viewed from within the conservatory. As such, a Japanese garden and placid water lily garden were designed and built here. In an effort to attract youngsters to the world of horticulture, Phipps added an outdoor children's garden in recent years, animating the space with loud colors and playful exhibits, allowing the conservatory to thrive and maintain its stunning architectural setting.

OPPOSITE

TOP: *Crowds welcome the conservatory's spring display.*
BOTTOM: *Steamy warmth inside the conservatory contrasts with cold but beautiful new snow.*

YEAR OPENED
1893–1902

HEIGHT
64 feet

AREA
43,493 square feet

CONSERVATORY HOURS
Tuesday–Sunday 9:00 a.m. to 5:00 p.m.; Closed Mondays, Thanksgiving Day, and Christmas Day

LOCATION
One Schenley Park
Pittsburgh, PA 15213

FURTHER INFORMATION
(412) 622-6914
www.phipps.conservatory.org

Biltmore Estate Conservatory

ASHEVILLE, NORTH CAROLINA

The Biltmore Estate conservatory was an important part of George W. Vanderbilt's elaborate vision for his North Carolina estate. Built as a collaboration between architect Richard Morris Hunt and landscape architect Frederick Law Olmsted, the conservatory sits at the south end of the estate's vast gardens, below the line of sight from the 250-room mansion so that views from the latter remain uninterrupted.

The north façade of the steel and glass Lord & Burnham showpiece includes arched windows and doorways fashioned in bricks made from clay found on the original 125,000-acre estate. An unusual feature of the conservatory is the twelve-thousand-square-foot basement that housed the boiler, coal storage, gardeners' workrooms, and equipment areas. Outdoor walkways between the wings of the 7,500-square-foot conservatory incorporate skylights to brighten the workspace below.

More than a century of watering plants in the conservatory created inevitable problems as moisture, fertilizers, and other chemicals seeped into the foundation between the main floor and the basement. In 1997, the estate closed the conservatory for a two-year intensive restoration, recreating the original masterpiece, while updating the building with advanced climate control, new wiring and plumbing, and an efficient boiler with hot water heating. Fifty percent of the ventilation systems are now automatic; the rest retain

OPPOSITE: *The glass roof and brick front were erected as a collaboration between the architect and the landscape architect.*

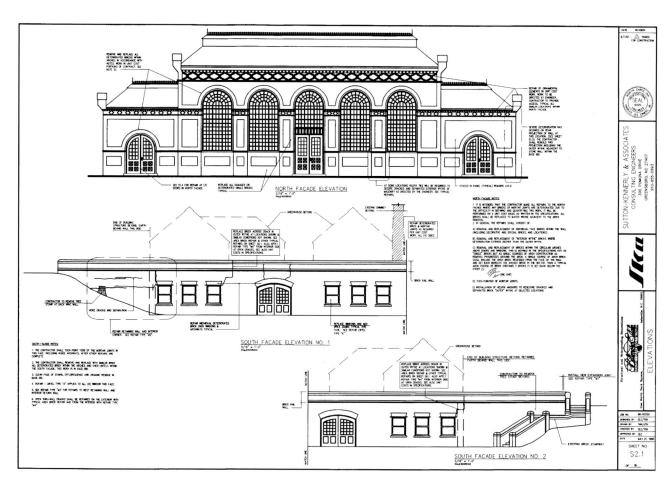

ABOVE: *Architectural elevations show the large basement area.*
RIGHT: *Plants within the conservatory are similar to those in Vanderbilt's original collection.*

*Archways over doors and
windows repeat the pat-
tern used in the mansion.*

The English Walled Garden in the 1930s, when roses were grown in elaborate arches and floral Maypoles.

their original iron manual cranks in case of power failure. Concrete and asphalt walkways from a 1950s reconstruction were ripped out and replaced by brick paths that match existing architectural elements of the building.

In keeping with late-nineteenth-century display philosophy, only two soil beds in the conservatory have plants directly in the ground: the Hot House and Cool House. All other plants grow in containers on benches. In some areas, flowering and foliage varieties do double duty as part of the conservatory's display and for use in the main house. Huge potted plants rotate between Biltmore House's Winter Garden and the glasshouse; the conservatory also grows thousands of bedding plants that go in the gardens around the estate.

Vanderbilt's original plants in the Palm House showed his determination to have a far-reaching horticultural display with such specimens as Red Latan Palms from the Reunion Islands, African Senegal Date Palms, Tasmanian Tree Ferns from Australia, and Bamboo Palms from China. None of the original plants remains in the Palm House, but today's collection has many of the same varieties of palms along with changing groups of understory plants that range from background greenery like ferns to showy anthuriums. The Hot House displays tropical flowering plants, and the Cool House contains subtropical and temperate plants such as gardenias, camellias, and citrus trees. Additional rooms hold orchids and bromeliads, cacti, and succulents. An Exhibition Room features educational displays that change several times a year; the Propagation Room shows flowers and plants growing in the estate's production facility.

YEAR OPENED
1893

HEIGHT
40 feet

AREA
7,500 square feet

CONSERVATORY HOURS
Daily 9:00 a.m. to 5:00 p.m., January–March;
Daily 8:30 a.m. to 5:00 p.m. (open until 6:00 p.m. during Daylight Savings Time), April–December;

Closed Thanksgiving Day and Christmas Day

LOCATION
U.S. Highway 25
Asheville, NC 28801

FURTHER INFORMATION
(800) 543-2961
www.biltmore.com

The Dorrance H. Hamilton Fernery

THE MORRIS ARBORETUM OF THE UNIVERSITY OF PENNSYLVANIA,

PHILADELPHIA, PENNSYLVANIA

The Morris Arboretum was planned and developed in 1887 by John and Lydia Morris, siblings from a prominent Quaker family. In the course of their education, the Morrises spent considerable time in Europe absorbing the culture of the Old World, amid grand villas and their magnificent gardens. Upon their return the Morrises designed a garden modeled, unsurprisingly, upon Victorian tastes. The overall composition of the arboretum, now owned by the University of Pennsylvania, reads more as a testament to the Morrises' eclectic personal tastes than to any specific design school.

John was particularly taken with the conservatories that he visited in Europe and in 1899 he designed a fernery for a focused plant collection. The octagonal structure, sunken below grade in order to maintain the precise level of humidity and temperature necessary for propagating ferns in this climate, was based upon examples John observed in England. Using no support poles, Morris designed the roof as a flowing curvature of glass, but then "relieved the spectator from the impression that he is walking under glass" by placing wrought iron braces at points along the surface. After a hundred years, the Dorrance H. Hamilton Fernery, as it is known today, is the only remaining free-standing fernery in North America.

To create the distinctive subterranean grotto ambiance, Morris hired Japanese

OPPOSITE: *The Hamilton Fernery is below grade to maintain the proper climactic levels for the ferns.*

The modern fernery receives shade from nearby tall trees; inside, taller plants shade the more sensitive understory growth.

Growing directly on rocks, the Bear's Paw fern, Aglaoamorpha meyeniana, *has both fertile parts and sterile parts on the same frond and fuzzy brown rhizomes that suggest its name.*

ABOVE: *The Hamilton Fernery is the only remaining free-standing fernery in North America.*
RIGHT: *Restoration for the fernery replaced the old iron heating pipes along the side and revealed the grotto in the original rockwork.*

garden makers Kushibiki and Arai to arrange one hundred tons of local Wissahickon schist into rockery formations resembling a cave or mountain cliff accented by delicate waterfalls, a flowing stream bed, and a goldfish pond. Once the plants took hold on the rocky surfaces, entering the fernery felt like a journey through a personal terrarium.

The original collection of about one thousand ferns, representing 523 different varieties, was purchased from the Manchester, England firm of J & W Burkenhead. In its prime, the Morrises' fernery had one of the finest displays of filmy ferns (*Hymenophyllacae*) in cultivation—a difficult feat considering the species' delicate nature and requirements of 100 percent humidity but no direct water. Today's plant collection includes temperate ferns that can survive temperatures as low as fifty degrees on winter nights and above one hundred degrees in steamy Philadelphia summers. Interesting

specimens include the Bear's Paw fern that is endemic to the Philippines and Taiwan (*Aglaoamorpha meyeniana*). This exotic specimen has both its fertile parts and sterile parts occupying the same frond and fuzzy brown rhizomes that suggest its name.

A 1997 architectural renovation, spearheaded by funding from local philanthropist Dorrance H. Hamilton, saw stainless steel and aluminum roof supports substituted for the original iron. However, the cast iron heating pipes that run in parallel around the interior perimeter of the wall are exact replicas of the originals, except that today's pipes use recycled hot water controlled by computers rather than steam powered by pressure.

The Dorrance H. Hamilton Fernery is one of the few remaining ferneries in the United States, and is a magnificent timepiece, a tribute to pteridomania or "fern mania" that gripped the Victorian imagination during the golden age of conservatories in the late-nineteenth century.

YEAR OPENED
1899

HEIGHT
23 feet

AREA
1,261 square feet

CONSERVATORY HOURS
Monday–Friday 10:00 a.m. to 4:00 p.m., Saturday and Sunday 10:00 a.m. to 5:00 p.m., April–October; Saturday and Sunday 10:00 a.m. to 4:00 p.m., November–March

LOCATION
100 Northwestern Avenue
Philadelphia, PA 19118

FURTHER INFORMATION
(215) 247-5777
www.upenn.edu/morris

Enid A. Haupt Conservatory

THE NEW YORK BOTANICAL GARDEN, BRONX, NEW YORK

ↄ ↄ

*L*ike many conservatories, the New York Botanical Garden's original glasshouse suffered from nearly a century of neglect and questionable renovations in 1938 and 1956, when ornamental entranceways and other indications of the Italian Renaissance influence were removed. By the late 1970s, the city considered demolishing the building, but Enid A. Haupt stepped up and began a rescue effort that continued until 1997.

In the early nineteen nineties, the conservatory closed for an extensive four-year restoration, propelled by funds from the city and a generous donation from Haupt, a former president of the American Horticultural Society. Although remaining faithful to the original design, modeled after European conservatories like the one at the Royal Botanic Gardens at Kew near London, and implemented by Lord & Burnham in 1899, the restoration required the replacement of almost all the glazing, an update of the entire mechanical system, and a reconsideration of the plant collection.

During restoration, the design of the plant collection took on a whole new look. Until 1992 the plants were arranged in the traditional botanical fashion, separated by family and type, representative of the Victorian way of viewing the natural world. The new design mimics the way that nature actually works. So, within the various rooms that comprise the major exhibit, called "A World

OPPOSITE: *The impeccably restored Enid A. Haupt Conservatory, designed in a modernized Italian Renaissance style, is an officially dedicated New York City Landmark.*

{55}

ABOVE: *Covered with epiphytes, the fallen portion of a reconstructed kapok tree is the dominant feature in the Tropical Lowland Rain Forest Gallery.*
RIGHT: *Aquatic plants flourish both inside and out.*

LEFT: *An unusual double-trunked Boojum tree,* Fouquieria columnaris, *reigns over the Deserts of the Americas Gallery.*
RIGHT: *A high-pressure mist system adds to the tropical atmosphere.*

of Plants," visitors traverse an entire planet of ecosystems from lowland to upland tropical rainforests, from desert flora in Africa to that of the Americas. In each instance, the display is arranged to be as naturalistic as possible, with fallen trees lying across the ground and plants left to grow where they might. Not that the presentation isn't carefully edited and maintained. But the idea is to do so not with a Linnean concept of dividing each specimen from another, but with the ecological concept of seeing the entire presentation as a whole.

Visitors enter the conservatory under the towering dome of the Palms of the Americas Gallery to see the world's most extensive greenhouse collection of palms that are native to the Western Hemisphere. From here, visitors move into the biome of a tropical lowland rainforest dominated by a model of a full-sized fallen kapok tree (*Ceiba pentandra*) covered with living epiphytes. Vanilla vine and other flowering orchids, flowering bromeliads, and other epiphytic plants vie for growing space between the thick roots of a massive old philodendron winding around the trunk of the kapok. Throughout the collection are numerous endangered species such as the chocolate tree (*Theobroma cacao*).

In addition to the natural elements there are many subtle design gestures that are perfectly knitted into the overall fabric without being ostentatious. One of these, a raised bluestone pool of aquatic plants, acts as a transition to the Tropical Upland Rainforest exhibit. Terraced rockwork provides a growing space for ferns, moss, lichen, and orchids that thrive in cooler, high-altitude temperatures. Besides the beauty, the garden aims to educate, and many of the individual displays contain intriguing examples of natural processes. For instance, within the extensive exhibit of desert ecosystems, sits the towering skeleton of an old cactus, revealing the amazing architecture that makes up the plant's water storage system. Another display contrasts New World genera with plants of the Old World, graphically illustrating the process of adaptation.

With the exception of occasional waterfalls, the conservatory is a quiet place with a museum-like quality, enhanced by the way that some of the rarer specimens are exhibited. Many orchids, for example, reside within climate-controlled glass cases. An emphasis on educating the visitor about conservation and the role plants play in human life is evident throughout the conservatory. Inside a replica of a tropical rainforest healer's hut, garden docents give a quick lecture on medicinal plants, using samples from the garden's world-renowned herbarium.

A gallery of magnificent hanging baskets leads to the final section of the conservatory, devoted to seasonal displays. During the spring, the space is a kaleidoscope of bulbs in bloom and flowering shrubs; in the summer it shifts to annuals and in the fall to chrysanthemums. The most popular show occurs during the winter holidays, when thousands of poinsettias nestle among a tapestry of permanently planted evergreen shrubs and trees. During this month-long presentation, miniature trains snake along a thousand-foot track over water, around hillsides, across an overhead trestle, and past small-scale New York landmarks. The buildings are exquisitely crafted from natural materials like twigs, bark, nuts and seeds, and they range from an eight-foot-long replica of the conservatory itself, to such famous New York houses as Edgar Alan Poe's tiny cottage.

OPPOSITE

The Palms of the Americas Gallery houses the world's most extensive glasshouse collection of palms from both North and South America.

YEAR OPENED
1900

HEIGHT
90 feet

AREA
55,000 square feet

CONSERVATORY HOURS
Tuesday–Sunday and Monday holidays, 10:00 a.m. to 6:00 p.m., April–October; 10:00 a.m. to 4:00 p.m., November–March; Closed Mondays, Thanksgiving Day, and Christmas Day

LOCATION
200th Street and Kazimiroff Boulevard Bronx, NY 10458-5126

FURTHER INFORMATION
(718) 817-8700
www.nybg.org

Sonnenberg Conservatory Range

SONNENBERG GARDENS, CANANDAIGUA, NEW YORK

The conservatory range at Sonnenberg Gardens is part of an impressive private estate built by Mary Clark and Frederick Ferris Thompson between 1863 and 1923. Mrs. Thompson was a patron of the arts, including architecture and garden design, and she commissioned landscape architect Ernest Bowditch, a protégé of Frederick Law Olmsted, to design the sumptuous formal gardens that surround the manse. In addition to these, Thompson had a series of conservatories designed and built by Lord & Burnham. When Mrs. Thompson was at her home in New York City during the winter, as special messenger traveled by train several times a week to deliver flowers and fruit from her greenhouses. Production was so vast that wagonloads of fruit and vegetables from the greenhouses in winter and from the gardens in summer went to nearby F.F. Thompson Hospital and Clark Manor House, both of which considered the Thompsons their chief benefactors.

Lord & Burnham spent a decade constructing all the houses, using a limestone knee wall, supporting iron framework, and old-growth cypress crossbeams as structural materials throughout. The glasswork was intricately formed for each change of the geometry, including many panes that were curved to fit the roof bars. Each house had specialized interior construction to accommodate the plants within. Wires were strung along the glass ceilings of the vineries and

OPPOSITE: *The Sonnenberg greenhouse range is one of the few remaining examples of the extensive glasshouses originally built for private use.*

melon houses in order to support grapevines and casaba melons; netting was hung under the wires to catch falling fruit. The rose house's tiered benches of soil beds with tile bottoms and wooden sides allowed for better air circulation than traditional, single-level benches.

After Mary Clark Thompson's death in 1923, the conservatory and gardens declined until the 1970s. Since then, the important structural changes in the conservatory complex have entailed a new heating system, replacement of many pieces of frosted glass, and upgrades for the progressively deteriorating wooden crossbeams.

The main feature of the conservatory is still the palm house, devoted primarily to tropical plants. In addition to a fountain and koi pool, the space sports an unusual wall made of porous tufa rock covered with plants like ferns, well-suited to life in the lime-rich stone pockets.

The former vinery is now a gift shop and admissions area, while the peach and nectarine houses have become a restaurant. But the most significant change is the transformation of two of the largest houses into space devoted to children, complemented by an outdoor garden for kids. The Children's Education Building, resembling a barn with skylights, developed as a result of Sonnenberg's original modest program for youngsters from ages six to eleven. After only two years the program expanded considerably to include classes in cooperation with the local Canandaigua School District, vacation classes for children of all ages, and requests from a number of nearby universities for advanced-level classes in horticulture.

From the orchid show and bulb show in spring through the chrysanthemum display and holiday festival of lights, the conservatory attracts a continuous following, but it closes in winter to avoid the heavy costs associated with heating buildings and snow plowing miles of roads and walkways around the fifty-acre estate.

OPPOSITE

TOP: *Greenhouse flowers.*

BOTTOM RIGHT: *Sonnenberg's Palm dome is an elegant reminder of Victorian times in the midst of a huge range of functional greenhouses.*

BOTTOM LEFT: *Original tufa rock wall.*

YEAR OPENED
1903

HEIGHT
30 feet

AREA
13,000 square feet

CONSERVATORY HOURS
Open every day 9:30 a.m. to 5:30 p.m., mid-May to mid-October

LOCATION
151 Charlotte Street
Canandaigua, 14424

FURTHER INFORMATION
(716) 394-4922
www.sonnenberg.org

Volunteer Park Conservatory

VOLUNTEER PARK, SEATTLE, WASHINGTON

Volunteer Park was designed by the Olmsted Brothers of Brookline, Massachusetts, the company formed by Frederick Law Olmsted, designer of New York's Central Park, Boston's Emerald Necklace, and a plethora of urban landscapes across the country. In carrying on their father's practice, Olmsted's sons maintained a similar aesthetic, derived from the English garden park style. Today Volunteer Park remains one of the best-preserved of the Olmsted city landscapes.

In 1912, Seattle's Department of Parks and Recreation purchased a conservatory kit, from New York's Hitchings & Company, and erected it at the north end of Volunteer Park. The structural frame of the conservatory was made of steel, although the graceful roof arches originally were built with Southern swamp cypress. In spite of persistent dampness, both inside and out, the cypress lasted for seventy-five years, when it was replaced in the mid 1980s with Alaskan white cedar. The most recent renovation, finished in late 1999, replaced all existing wood with aluminum and removed all the single pane glazing in favor of annealed glass.

Just below the vestibule ceiling hangs a beautiful interior glass canopy created by Seattle glass artist Richard Spaulding titled "Homage in Green" (1982), with lilies and passion flowers etched in the center. The work follows the Victorian tradition of using architectural ornamentation to carry the narrative motif of a building.

OPPOSITE: *After decades of disrepair, Seattle's magnificent conservatory once again presides over the city from atop Capitol Hill.*

ABOVE: *By 1920, Seattle's Volunteer Park Conservatory had both bench displays and landscaped exhibits, while they maintained traditional linear layouts.*

RIGHT: *A beveled glass lunette above the entrance, and the green glass canopy just inside the doors, were the only additions during the renovation.*

ABOVE: *The Seasonal Display House uses backbone plants that are hardy in the Pacific Northwest to show off changing displays of seasonal color.*

LEFT: *The conservatory's orchid collection contains over a thousand specimens.*

ABOVE: *Richard Spaulding's stained glass canopy,* Homage in Green, *traces three hundred years of architectural ornamentation in thirty-five perimeter panels. The center of the canopy features lilies, convolvuli, and passionflowers etched in the Victorian tradition.*
RIGHT: *The Fern House includes a pond with* monstera *overhang.*

The conservatory is divided into five different houses: the Palm House, Cactus and Succulent House, Fern House, Bromeliad House, and the Seasonal Display House. The names are generally descriptive of their contents, though many other subcollections appear throughout. Around the perimeter of the Palm House, for instance, is an ever-changing orchid display. The orchid collection was started in 1921 and today contains over a thousand specimens, many of which are divisions of the original plants, including epiphytic and terrestrial orchids of the Pacific Northwest. The Fern House proudly displays cycads, ferns, and the giant Mexican breadfruit, a fragrant philodendron called *Monstera deliciosa*. The Bromeliad House does a good job explaining the nature of bromeliads like pineapples and other epiphytes, and they maintain a particularly excellent collection of tillandsias.

From the beginning, the conservatory's mission was to collect and conserve threatened plants, a philosophy that continues today. Volunteer Park Conservatory serves as a plant-rescue site for exotics seized by the U.S. Department of Agriculture/Fish and Wildlife. As one of about fifty institutions that are members of CITES, the Convention on International Trade in Endangered Species, the conservatory provides a haven for plants that come from U.S. ports of entry, where they failed to meet import requirements that can range from infected by disease to illegal, endangered, or threatened. The plants go in quarantine for thirty days, during which time their country of origin may reclaim them, and then they go on display to the public. Part of the rescue-site agreement provides that the plants must remain in the designated institution forever and may never be traded or sold. Volunteer Park Conservatory has received about eight hundred plants since 1992. The building also fills a vital role in community botanical education with a variety of classes geared to horticulturists and to the amateur gardener.

YEAR OPENED
1912

HEIGHT
35 feet

AREA
6,000 square feet

CONSERVATORY HOURS
Daily 10:00 a.m. to 4:00 p.m., including holidays; 10:00 a.m. to 7:00 p.m., Memorial Day–Labor Day

LOCATION
1400 East Galer Street Seattle, WA 98112

FURTHER INFORMATION
(206) 684-4743
www.ci.seattle.wa.us/parks/ parkspaces/Volprkco.htm

Como Park Conservatory

COMO PARK, ST. PAUL, MINNESOTA

German-born Frederick Nussbaumer worked at the Royal Botanic Gardens at Kew outside of London as a young boy. In the 1880s he met the landscape architect Horace W. Cleveland, who at the time was putting the finishing touches on the Twin Cities' park system. At Cleveland's urging Nussbaumer came to the United States and eventually worked his way up to superintendent of the Twin Cities parks. For twenty years he tried to replace the basic municipal greenhouse with a structure befitting a city on the rise, something like the great Victorian glasshouse he had known at Kew. Finally, in 1915, the city commissioned King Construction Co. of Tonawanda, New York, to build an elegant wood and glass

conservatory, which Nussbaumer filled with palms, ferns, oversized water platters, and other popular Victorian collectibles.

Time and the bitter northern climate, combined with declining public interest, saw the structure deteriorate and the plant collection decline. A 1962 hailstorm shattered massive amounts of glass and drew attention to the need for improvements. In 1983 a major restoration began and took almost a decade to complete. Today, the reconstructed Como Park Conservatory consists of more than a half-acre of displays under an improved structure of aluminum, steel, and glass. Further alterations in 1998 resulted in an innovative water management system, hailed by environmentalists for its forward-

OPPOSITE: *Popular events at the Como Park Conservatory warm cold winters in St. Paul.*

ABOVE: *Looking toward the Palm dome, the Sunken Garden camouflages its elevators to look like planter boxes brimming with pink flowers, here on the center right side.*

RIGHT: *Harriet Frishmuth's sculpture* Play Days *draws attention to the soothing water feature in Como's Sunken Garden.*

ABOVE: *A vintage car and tents are part of the celebration at the 1998 opening of the restored veranda and plaza at Como.*

LEFT: *An early postcard shows the realization of Frederick Nussbaumer's dream.*

thinking approach. Gutters added to the roofline collect rainwater that goes to underground cisterns. The rainwater, free of the chemical additives found in city water, is pumped back to the conservatory, heated to 70 degrees, then applied to the tropical plants. Excess water flows through storm ceptors that divert the water to a frog pond in Como Park.

In the early 1980s, before the ADA requirement led many conservatories to add elevators, Como installed hydraulic lifts between the gallery and the main floor of the Sunken Garden, where they put on five seasonal flower shows annually. Because the interior architectural elements occur in twos, like the twin marble staircases, they installed two lifts, customed designed to look like planters and flanked by plants that help them blend beautifully into the surroundings.

The main Palm Dome holds orchids, bromeliads, and a growing collection of temperate understory palms. Two noteworthy orchids bear the names *Rossioglossum insleayi*

'Como Conservation' and *Masillaria pseudoreichenhamiana* 'Como Conservatory.'

The North Garden appeals to all ages with educational displays of plants that have a human use, whether it is for food or industry, or even those that are spiritual, cultural and social in nature. The Gallery Garden reinforces the conservatory's art classes by displaying works of art in conjunction with decorative flora, and the bonsai room reinforces the history of the collection.

Many cities have built their glasshouses and zoos in the same park, but St. Paul does one of the best jobs of coordinating the two. A prime example is their popular annual conservatory show about animals in the rainforest.

Every February, in conjunction with the adjacent Como Park Zoo, the conservatory puts on a ten-day lecture series about animals of the rainforest, where they brings bats and other small rainforest creatures to the tropical exhibit in the conservatory, demonstrating the plant/animal interactions and how each evolved.

OPPOSITE

Ornamental entryways on the wings provide a buffer zone against the cold.

YEAR OPENED
1915

HEIGHT
64 feet

AREA
26,000 square feet

CONSERVATORY HOURS
Daily 10:00 a.m. to 4:00 p.m., October–March; 10:00 a.m. to 6 :00 p.m., April–September 30

LOCATION
1325 Aida Place
St. Paul, MN 55103

FURTHER INFORMATION
(651) 487-8200
www1.stpaul.gov/ parksrec/conserv.html

The Conservatory at Longwood Gardens

LONGWOOD GARDENS, KENNETT SQUARE, PENNSYLVANIA

Young Pierre S. Du Pont was dazzled by the conservatories, gardens, and fountains he saw on his travels through Europe and then at the World's Fairs in Philadelphia (1876), Paris (1889), and Chicago (1893). The extravagant presentations inspired Du Pont to dream about building his own conservatory, when he wrote in 1918, "my ideas are quite beyond ordinary greenhouse construction . . . designed to exploit the sentiments and ideas associated with plants and flowers in a large way."

Du Pont's concept of "garden as theater" led to the development of 1,050 acres of magnificent horticulture, architecture, music, and theater when he purchased Pierce's Park in 1906, changed the name to Longwood, and began to realize his dream. The massive beaux-arts style concrete and glass conservatory, planned by Alexander J. Harper and completed by J. Walter Cope, opened on November 25, 1921. Over the years, constant alterations have perpetuated Du Pont's vision of horticultural presentations.

Today's conservatory covers four acres and includes extensive production houses and a courtyard summer display of waterlilies and waterplatters sturdy enough to hold children.

The main hall, known as the Orangery, first held orange trees, but when they failed to produce enough fruit, they were removed. Now the space features perfect lawns surrounded by waves of flowers in bloom and flanked by twenty-five-foot-tall concrete

OPPOSITE: *Longwood Conservatory's waterlily display holds more than one hundred different day- and night-blooming aquatic plants, including huge hybrid waterplatters developed at Longwood for their red color and tolerance to cold weather.*

RIGHT: *Nine new production greenhouses, covering thirty thousand square feet, supply ideal conditions for plants like these chrysanthemums to become part of the magic at Longwood.*

ABOVE: *Longwood's holiday season warms the heart with elegant plants, whimsical character exhibits, and millions of lights on trees outside.*

*Lily ponds, both inside and out, are a
popular feature in conservatories.*

TOP LEFT: *Longwood excels in the use of interior lawns for elegant contrast to seasonal flowers.*
BOTTOM LEFT: *The Mediterranean Garden celebrates plants that grow in climates with moist, cool winters and hot, dry summers.*
RIGHT: *Five orchid houses grow 7,500 plants, from which a few hundred in perfect bloom go on display to the public.*

columns covered with creeping fig (*Ficus pumila*). A central walkway leads to the Exhibition Hall designed around a rectangular shallow plane of water and flanked with Australian tree ferns (*Sphaeropteris cooperi*). As a reminder of Du Pont's days of lavish entertaining, Longwood still boasts a ballroom with a sonorous 10,010 pipe Aeolian organ that was custom-built in 1929.

The original Azalea House was replaced in 1973 by the rolling landscapes of the East Conservatory, a fifty-foot-high domed space covered by a free-span acrylic lamella arch roof. In 2001, the East Conservatory dome will be replaced with a more traditional ridge and furrow roof constructed of steel and glass above a new, exotic landscape. Some of the most popular exhibits are the restful Silver Garden, the expanded indoor Children's Garden sparkling with interactive fountains and mazes, and the tropical Cascade Garden, a collaboration between Roberto Burle Marx and Conrad Hamerman.

The sophisticated elegance and understated dignity of the conservatory is part of its theatrical effect. To preserve the idyllic illusion, a maze of tunnels runs beneath the walkways with miles of pipes, wires, and valves that support mechanical systems. Seventy cast iron radiators hang in the tunnels, just below the walkway grating, providing heat for the rooms above. To further insure a perfect landscape, a complete root zone heating system lies twenty-six inches below the planting beds so that room temperatures can be kept cool at night, preserving the flowers longer.

Seasonal productions dazzle visitors with masterpieces like the autumn celebration using twenty-thousand chrysanthemums, including everything from topiaries and bonsai to stunning hanging globes more than five feet in diameter. The most popular display occupies the last month of the year, when two thousand poinsettias set the atmosphere for lavish, magical sets that recreate the excitement and beauty of the season.

Longwood Gardens continues Pierre Du Pont's dream of theatrical garden productions. During the summer months, an incredible fountain, fireworks, and music concert series takes place in the Main Fountain Garden along the south side of the Conservatory. In the winter, the Conservatory's dramatic displays warm visitors with an elegant taste of Old World glamour.

YEAR OPENED
1921

HEIGHT
40 feet

AREA
100,000 square feet

CONSERVATORY HOURS
10:00 a.m. to 6:00 p.m., April–October; 10:00 a.m. to 5:00 p.m., November–March, open until 9:00 p.m. during Christmas display (Thanksgiving to early January)

LOCATION
P.O. Box 501
Kennett Square, PA
19348-0501

FURTHER INFORMATION
(610) 388-1000
www.longwoodgardens.org

United States Botanic Garden Conservatory

A national garden was first proposed by George Washington as an important component of the Federal infrastructure. Thomas Jefferson and then James Madison revived the notion, adding that the intelligence of the American people would be greatly enhanced by a museum devoted to the natural world. Although it took over a hundred years for this idea to be implemented, the concept has grown and the public has embraced it. In the same way that natural history museums around the country have evolved from static displays to interactive experiences, the USBG's shining new conservatory attracts all ages with energetic, thoughtful, interesting exhibits.

The original United States Botanic Garden Conservatory, constructed in 1933, was the first large structure ever to use aluminum as a building material. The ubiquitous greenhouse construction firm of Lord & Burnham used thirty-three tons of aluminum in conjunction with 276 tons of steel to erect a magnificent dome over Washington's then diminutive skyline. With an early awareness of safety precautions, they also installed wire-embedded glass in portions of the roof.

But time and the elements took their toll, necessitating a major restoration. Completed in 2000, this effort restored the historic limestone facade of the building. Beyond this, almost everything is new under the glass and steel superstructure. In addition to the

OPPOSITE: *The USBG Conservatory was the first building to use alumimun as a structural material.*

*From the street front, the USBG's
conservatory dome barely shows
above the somber government facade.*

Historic plants such as this
Encephalartos horridus, *from*
an early Wilkes expedition, continue
to augment the conservatory's
collection.

The USBG Conservatory (shown
before the 2000 renovation) rivals
the Capitol dome for majestic exteriors.

splendid, airy Palm House, two new houses and a new lobby were built to expand the displays and provide more space for service areas and for the public. The designers added cutting-edge computerized environmental systems that balance temperature, shade, humidity, and ventilation to keep plants growing and visitors comfortable.

Exhibits in the west half of the conservatory were chosen for their importance to people. Case study exhibits reveal how plants have been used in industry, medicine, and the arts. The conservatory's east half explores ecology and the evolutionary biology of plants. Themes in the adjoining houses include a Jurassic landscape with primitive plants like cycads, an ecological display of plant adaptations, an oasis, and desert plants.

The Palm House is a recreated jungle as it might have evolved from an abandoned plantation in a tropical rainforest; the two interior courtyards serve as a children's garden and as a contemplation garden. With great care, historic plants like the Ferocious Blue cycad (*Encephalartos horridus*) from Charles Wilkes' 1838–42 expedition, were saved from the original conservatory and continue to be displayed.

The Rare and Endangered Species House makes clear the urgent need to protect plants that are threatened by the destruction of their habitat for development and by wild collection for commercial trade. Visitors learn about plant protection activities arising from political agreements (CITES), plant rescue sites, and other national and international organizations.

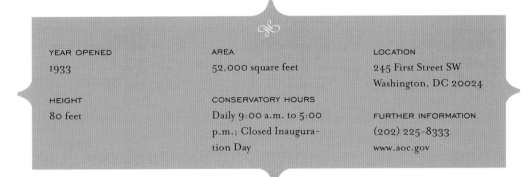

YEAR OPENED
1933

HEIGHT
80 feet

AREA
52,000 square feet

CONSERVATORY HOURS
Daily 9:00 a.m. to 5:00 p.m.; Closed Inauguration Day

LOCATION
245 First Street SW
Washington, DC 20024

FURTHER INFORMATION
(202) 225-8333
www.aoc.gov

Conservatory in Eden Park, Cincinnati, Ohio

13 AT 196

Irwin M. Krohn Conservatory

Cincinnati's Krohn Conservatory is one of the few remaining examples of glasshouses built in parks in the 1930s. The Art Deco influence resounds in the brilliant graphic design carved into the terrazzo floor, as well as in the etched flowers and leaves that adorn the glass panels at the entrance. The floral motif extends further to colorful stained glass depicting garden scenes, and then is repeated as molded metal panels found along a metal stair railing.

Eden Park, the conservatory's home, has had a municipal greenhouse or conservatory since the mid-1880s. During the last part of the nineteenth century these were utilitarian structures, used to propagate up to a quarter of a million plants annually for public dis-play throughout the city. At the turn of the century the desire to have a significant enclosed public garden gripped the city, resulting in the development of a new green-house for public flower shows. But it was not until 1933 that the city parks system finally built the impressive structure we see today, designed by architects Rapp and Meachem and dedicated in honor of park commis-sioner Irwin M. Krohn.

Unlike many glasshouses, the Krohn Conservatory has remained well kept over the years. The conservatory closed briefly after a massive storm in the summer of 1966, then again in 1970. The architectural firm Lord & Burnham assessed the damage, removed more than fourteen tons of broken glass, and

OPPOSITE: *A souvenir postcard depicts Krohn Conservatory just after it was built in the early 1930s.*

ABOVE: *Krohn is just one of several conservatories with a summer butterfly show, which attracts thousands of visitors.*

RIGHT: *Tropical House greenery flourishes, even after the summer of 1970 when the plants stood outside for months while the conservatory was completely rebuilt.*

TOP: *Holiday displays include festive flowers and a model train set, complete with overhead trestle.*
BOTTOM: *Art Deco flowers and leaves etched in glass adorn panels around the entrance.*

replaced the wooden superstructure with aluminum in 1970.

Today's conservatory space features tropical plants, a desert garden, a constantly changing orchid display, the Palm House, and the Floral Display House. A twenty-foot waterfall cascades over layers of native limestone into a stream that runs the length of the Palm House under a tropical flourish of palms, ferns, vines, and epiphytes. Tropical plants of economic value are part of the display, including food products like dwarf bananas, chocolate, starfruit, and vanilla pods. The desert garden showcases cacti and succulents from around the world, including a notable collection of aloes, agaves, and haworthias. Expanding the traditional concept of flower shows, Krohn's six annual shows include a sculpture show around Mother's Day and a popular summer butterfly extravaganza.

Reciprocal community involvement is an integral part of Krohn's success. Volunteers augment the small staff and cover many aspects of the conservatory, from maintaining the collections to educating the public.

OPPOSITE

TOP: *A Nativity scene, including live animals, has been a Christmas tradition at Krohn for years.*
BOTTOM: *Eden Park has had public greenhouses since the mid-1880s, not for architectural statements but for the enjoyment and education of the public.*

YEAR OPENED	AREA	LOCATION
1933	24,325 square feet	1501 Eden Park Drive Cincinnati, OH 45202
HEIGHT	CONSERVATORY HOURS	
45 feet	Daily 10:00 a.m. to 5:00 p.m.; Extended hours for seasonal shows	FURTHER INFORMATION (513) 421-5707 www.cinci-parks.org

Duke Gardens

Doris Duke was the independent daughter of tobacco tycoon James B. Duke, benefactor of Duke University. Known in her time as the richest woman in the world, she spent much of her private life traveling the globe in search of artifacts to augment collections that reflected interests in the fields of the art, music, nature, and historic preservation. Even though she had houses in California, Hawaii, New York, and Newport, Rhode Island, Miss Duke chose to develop her extensive gardens under glass at her 1912 birthplace in New Jersey.

Inspired by Longwood Gardens in nearby Pennsylvania, Duke built an elegant conservatory and filled it full of flowers she enjoyed for their color and fragrance, with little concern for their botanical classifications. Encouraged by Samuel Du Pont in the 1950s, she adopted Longwood's showcase philosophy, and the collection blossomed into a series of exotic garden settings contained within eleven interconnected glass houses. The show garden houses were built in a square formation with additional glass houses constructed inside the square for plant production and support.

Miss Duke's garden designs were based upon her personal impressions of cultural traditions from abroad, including Italian, English, French, Chinese, Japanese, and Indo-Persian landscapes, as well as more generally conceived orchid, desert, semi-tropical, and jungle environments. By 1964,

OPPOSITE: *Doris Duke decorated the entryway with an insignia of interlocking Ds.*

TOP: *A statue of a cherub stands in the middle of the succulents section of the English garden.*
BOTTOM: *A profusion of desert plants.*

TOP: *The French garden glows with seasonal flowers that are contained within a boxwood hedge in a fleur-de-lis pattern.*

BOTTOM: *The rose garden section of the Indo-Persian garden.*

Strict symmetry characterizes this
portion of the Indo–Persian garden.

she allowed private tours on a limited basis. After Doris Duke's death in 1993, Duke Gardens opened to the public, under a strict system of guided tours by reservation. No cars are allowed on the property; guests park in distant lots and then proceed to the private entrance via free bus service.

The gardens maintain consistent foundation and accent plantings such as the topiary animals, boxwood parterres, and ivy-covered columns in the French garden; otherwise brilliant annuals and perennials are changed four times a year, according to the seasons. Rather than focusing on plant species, Duke Gardens aims its scope more at making an artistic statement or aesthetic impression. The 1890s Edwardian Garden reminds guests of the Mauve Decade, when the passion was for orchids and pale mauve colors. The Colonial Garden features camellias, azaleas, magnolias, and crepe myrtle as they might grow in the South Atlantic states, where the Duke family originated. Elements of an Italian garden adorn the foyer. The Desert Garden resembles an American desert, although planted specimens come from beyond the continental United States.

Miss Duke applied the same poetic license to the structures themselves, an eclectic mixture of permanent and semipermanent greenhouses that emphasize ornamentation more than architecture. Hardscape interest in the French Garden, for example, focuses on three barrel vaults built with deep green lattice work in perfect accompaniment to the manicured parterres on the ground. Authentic wattle willow fencing brought from England frames the flowers in the English border garden.

YEAR OPENED
1964

HEIGHT
40 feet

AREA
30,000 square feet

CONSERVATORY HOURS
Daily Noon to 4:00 p.m., October–May; Closed June–September; Also closed Thanksgiving Day, Christmas Day, and New Year's Day; Guided tours required; Advance reservations requested; Reservation line open Monday–Friday 9:00 a.m. to 4:00 p.m.

LOCATION
Route 206 South
Somerville, NJ 08876

FURTHER INFORMATION
(908) 722-3700

Mitchell Park Horticultural Conservatory

MITCHELL PARK, MILWAUKEE, WISCONSIN

*I*n 1899, Milwaukee's oldest park erected a traditional conservatory that was popular but neglected in later years. The city razed the crumbling building in 1955 and joined the trend toward space age construction. Nothing was easy. The shapes were unique in the world of horticulture, so every system had to be custom designed. Cooling is accomplished by a fan system around the base and top of each dome that blows air in or out as needed; a complete air change can be made in only 3.5 minutes. Supersky Construction began the project in 1959, and finished the last dome in October 1967.

The three rounded conoidal domes of the Mitchell Park Conservatory, designed by Wisconsin architect Donald Grieb, differ from conventional geodesic configurations. The extra height of the beehive-shaped domes allows a better sun angle for winter solar heating and more room for tall trees. No steel is used at all; each dome has a concrete reinforced substructure of hexagons glazed with wire-embedded glass. And a built-in system of gutters along the glazing effectively eliminates interior condensation, collecting and funneling the water down through hollow aluminum tubing to the base of the dome.

Approximately four thousand plants brighten the domes with rotating flowers supplied by ten support greenhouses. Two domes have permanent displays, the third building changes its entire presentation five

OPPOSITE: *Mitchell Park's three beehive-shaped domes took their inspiration from geodesic configurations.*

*The Show Dome creates completely
new landscapes for the popular annual
Garden Railroad Show, run by a local
model train association.*

*Mitchell Park's original conservatory,
with wrought iron gates by artisan
Cyril Kolnick, stood from 1898 to
1955.*

*Historic props such as this wrought
iron gate from the original conservatory (shown in photos on the wall)
are cherished and reused as architectural accents in modern shows.*

times a year. The Arid Dome showcases desert plants grouped by geographic regions. In the center of the space lies a small oasis under towering date palms. Horticultural highlights include an impressive collection from Madagascar, with specimens like *pachypodium,* that looks like a spiney palm tree with white fragrant tips. The rest of the presentation shows cacti in a desert of the American Southwest, along with cacti and succulents from around the world. In an effort to mimic nature, the winter temperature in the Arid Dome hovers around fifty degrees, allowing the plants a dormant period with minimal watering.

Amidst the sounds of a waterfall and chattering birds, the Tropical Dome provides a beautiful, warm haven throughout the long Northern winter. Most noticeable is the giant, eighty-five-foot-tall kapok tree (*Ceiba pentandra*). The tree's stabilizing buttress roots demonstrate how the kapok adapted to the shallow soil beds of the tropical rainforest. Brilliantly colored orchids, bromeliads, and other tropicals animate the space, while some displays are designed according to use, such as the economic plants whose products enhance living throughout the world.

The third dome is devoted to a series of shows. More than the traditional flower extravaganzas, each show is a meticulously staged set with relevance to the local audience. For example, the conservatory has recently sponsored shows with titles like Indian Summer, recreating the daily life of the regional Native American woodland population, and an Oktoberfest complete with a huge bar laden with authentic German beer steins that celebrated Milwaukee's German heritage. The most popular event is the annual Garden Railroad Show with new themes every year from January to April. Throughout all three domes, birds, frogs, toads, fish, lizards, and turtles add to the naturalistic feeling with their background symphony of animal noises. Outside the conservatory lies a sunken garden that was originally designed in 1904 and is still well maintained.

YEAR OPENED
1964–67

HEIGHT
85 feet

AREA
15,393

CONSERVATORY HOURS
Daily 9:00 a.m. to 5:00 p.m.

LOCATION
524 South Layton Boulevard
Milwaukee, WI 53215

FURTHER INFORMATION
(414) 649-9830
www.countyparks.com/horticulture

Boettcher Memorial Conservatory

DENVER BOTANIC GARDENS, DENVER, COLORADO

Denver's 1966 conservatory is named after an early benefactor of the Denver Botanic Garden. Claude K. Boettcher was the founder of the Ideal Cement Company, and in tribute, the conservatory dome fretwork was made of reinforced concrete poured in place into wooden forms. The vaulted arch involved a laborious process that took ten months to complete.

A 1997 renovation replaced the dome's original glass with sturdier Plexiglas, and added state-of-the-art electrical and mechanical climate controls for heating, evaporative cooling, and general air circulation. A new reverse osmosis water purification system provides more than ten thousand gallons of water each day for irrigation and humidity that rival the tropics. Concrete pathways inside the structure enhance the forest effect with whimsical imprints of leaves and animal footprints. The winding paths and bridges over streams, past waterfalls and pools, and access to different heights, combined with extensive planting, makes visitors forget they are in a basic rectangular box. Focal points along the way can be as varied as a fossil zone or a subtle reminder about the endangered understory tropical chocolate tree, *Theobroma cacao.*

The centerpiece of the remodeling is a formidable cement replica of a lightning-damaged, sixty-five-year-old banyan tree rising forty feet above the Tropical Botanica display. Stairs corkscrew around the tree and

OPPOSITE: *The original glass in Boettcher's dome was replaced with Plexiglas in a recent renovation.*

{107}

TOP: *The distinctive fans of* Licuala ramsayi *draw the eye to an artificial crocodile.* BOTTOM: *Supported by massive buttress roots, an artificial banyan tree conceals elevator access to viewing platforms.*

The statue in the foreground, by artist Frank Swanson, is composed of three interlocking pieces of marble.

*View from the banyan tree's platform
to the pool below.*

a hidden elevator transports visitors above the conservatory floor to viewing platforms made of cypress logs. From here visitors can look down on the tropical tangle of palms, cycads, vines, ferns, and exotic flowers below. The tree itself features large buttress roots that extend out to the pond and actually help to create microclimates for growing epiphytes, orchids, bromeliads, aroids, and vines.

Unlike some conservatories, Boettcher changes the plants and their arrangement on a regular basis, to provide continuing excitement for visitors and for volunteers. The purpose of the tropical displays, both the rainforest and dry forest, is to educate as much as to entertain. Well written signs articulate the important role of plants in an ecosystem. Volunteers conduct theme tours and classes that stress the significance of medicinal and economic plants, conservation, plant communities, and ecology. For the self-guided tour, plants that demonstrate these concepts range from the Perfume Tree (*Cananga odorata*) used in Chanel No. 5 perfume, to Cinnamon (*Cinnamomum zeylanicum*) to Bay Rum (*Pimenta racemos*), and more. Boettcher Conservatory does a good job fulfilling its mission "to provide a basis for understanding the need for stewardship of tropical ecosystems and by extension, local ecosystems."

YEAR OPENED
1966

HEIGHT
51 feet

AREA
12,800 square feet

CONSERVATORY HOURS
Daily 9:00 a.m. to 5 :00 p.m.

LOCATION
1005 York Street
Denver, CO 80206

FURTHER INFORMATION
(303) 331-4000

Windows to the Tropics Conservatory

FAIRCHILD TROPICAL GARDEN, CORAL GABLES, MIAMI, FLORIDA

When he was only twenty-years old, plant explorer David Fairchild created the Section of Foreign Seed and Plant Introduction in the United States Department of Agriculture, then he spent the next thrity-seven years traveling the world in search of flora that could benefit his country. From his extensive voyages, he returned to the United States and introduced such important plants as alfalfa, mangos, dates, horseradish, and nectarines.

Colonel Robert Montgomery, a Florida businessman with a passion for plant collecting, decided to create a botanical garden in Miami, the one place in the continental United States where tropical plants could grow naturally outdoors. Opened in 1938, the Fairchild Tropical Garden was named in honor of the man who generously shared his experience and knowledge with Colonel Montgomery.

In addition to harboring a world-renown collection of tropical and subtropical palms, the Garden is an important player in conservation, exploration, and horticultural education. The Rare Plant House was built to protect the rare and tender tropical specimens that were too delicate to survive outdoors in the local subtropical climate, but Hurricane Andrew destroyed it in 1992. When supporters rebuilt the sheltered area, they created a new conservatory that opened in 1995, under a roof fabricated from nine thousand square feet of Suntuf, an unbreak-

OPPOSITE: *Fairchild's new conservatory has a better chance of surviving hurricanes.*

An interior view of the lower level of
Window Seven that explains plant-
animal interactions.

Colorful bromeliads highlight the
epiphyte exhibit.

able corrugated polycarbonate material, imported from Israel and twenty times stronger than common fiberglass. It is significant that the new conservatory's chief designers were horticulturists rather than architects.

Inside the building, visitors find lush verdant growth at every turn, even on the hand carved coral rock stairway covered with maidenhair ferns. The conservatory's theme, Windows to the Tropics, is organized into seven areas of interest, such as color association, diversity of form, ecological associations, and plant-animal interactions. The seven windows as a whole present an enlightened approach to understanding plant conservation that emphasizes not only its scientific aspects, but also the more subtle, aesthetic ones. Among the highlights of the collection are rare orchids, bromeliads, ferns, mosses, philodendrons, and an array of epiphytic cycads growing on an artificial tree, convincingly built with tubular cork bark affixed to PVC pipes.

The conservatory's endangered species collection glows with curiosities like *Musella lasiocarpa* (the first one of this banana-like plant that has bloomed in North America), a brilliant Red Sealing Wax Palm, *Cyrtostachys renda*, and gingers from China. Many conservatories boast of having one or two *Amorphophallus titanum* plants, the gigantic East Indian herb with a flower spike that reaches four feet in height, but Fairchild has forty different species of *Amorphophallus*.

At the forefront of responsible conservatory management, Fairchild deserves high praise for abandoning the use of chemicals in favor of Integrated Pest Management and for two underground cisterns that store forty-five thousand gallons of rainwater. They also make concerted efforts to reach out to the community, in the spirit of the best public conservatories of the Victorian era, welcoming visitors with bilingual brochures and signs in both English and Spanish.

OPPOSITE

LEFT: *Red sealing wax palms,* Crystostachys renda, *glow against tropical greenery.*
TOP RIGHT: Musella lasio-carpa, *the rare Chinese yellow flowered plant resembling a banana, grows both inside and outside the conservatory.*
BOTTOM RIGHT: *Window Two shows the wide variety of epiphytic plants, from Spanish moss to cactus and orchids.*

YEAR OPENED
1967 and 1995

HEIGHT
35 feet

AREA
16,000 square feet

CONSERVATORY HOURS
Daily 9:30 a.m. to 4:30 p.m.; Closed Christmas Day

LOCATION
10901 Cutler Road
Coral Gables, Miami,
FL 33156

FURTHER INFORMATION
(305) 667-1651
www.ftg.org

The John A. Sibley Horticultural Center

CALLAWAY GARDENS, PINE MOUNTAIN, GEORGIA

When it was erected in the mid-1980s, the John A. Sibley Horticultural Center was considered experimental. The structure is really half a structure, with little more than two thousand square feet of the plant collection under glass. The rest of it is partially or fully exposed to the elements. To achieve this, architects Craig, Gualden and Davis and landscape architect Robert Marvin worked closely and developed a system in which the plants and the structure are carefully interwoven so that delicate species have more shelter, and more resilient species receive greater exposure. There is a self-effacing nature to the design so that the transition from one microclimate to another appears to occur seamlessly, without human intervention. Partly this is due to the subdued character of the architecture, which promotes the visual physical flow between the indoor and outdoor settings—a rarity in traditional conservatories.

A curvilinear walkway and bedding scheme leads visitors on a meandering course through the five-acre display. In the absence of straight lines, the mind creates connections between spaces, moving from indoors to outdoors. Even the grassy area inside the structure extends to the outside lawn. To maintain growing temperatures in the inner enclosed areas, twenty-six glass folding doors, each twenty-four feet high and 1,600 pounds in weight, fold together across the open end of the conservatory to keep out

OPPOSITE: *The Sibley Center's design is innovative in that just two thousand square feet of the plant collection are under glass.*

The plants and the structure are carefully interwoven so that delicate species have more shelter, and more resilient species are allowed greater exposure.

ABOVE: *Delicately planted stone walls enhance the sound of the indoor waterfall,* Partners in Time.

OPPOSITE: *Stacked stone walls have planting pockets for both per-manent and rotating flower displays.*

Water, lawn, and flower features help eliminate boundaries by extending from inside to outside, through folding doors that are kept open for much of the year.

rain and cold during the short winter season from November to early March. Environmentally friendly designs eliminate the need for air conditioning. Deciduous trees on the south side provide shade in summer, while allowing light to warm the building in winter. Heat is dispersed with carefully placed fans, and evaporative cooling comes from multiple water features like the twenty-two-foot-high waterfall. Even the large, decorative wall of Tennessee fieldstone holds additional solar heat in the winter. The structure of the conservatory is fashioned from large thermal glass blocks; opaqe roof bubbles are made of a silicone-coated fiberglass fabric.

The planting design was carefully calculated to respond to the minute climatic changes that can occur within the space of a few feet, owing to sun aspect, shading, soil content, and wind patterns. These micro-climates exist everywhere but are not always considered when conservatories are designed. At the farthest fringes of the Sibley Center, the display is considered Georgian, where camellias dominate. Moving toward the interior, more delicate species emerge from a subtropical and borderline palette, filled with species that can grow if given even the slightest bit of shelter, such as a stone wall or overhang. Then the interior features traditional glasshouse varieties, such as tropical ferns, ficus, and hardy palms.

In another area of the fourteen-thousand-acre recreational complex that makes up Callaway Gardens is the popular Cecil B. Day Butterfly Center, one of the largest glass-enclosed butterfly conservatories in the United States. The octagonal structure is home to thousands of butterflies, including several rare species from Africa.

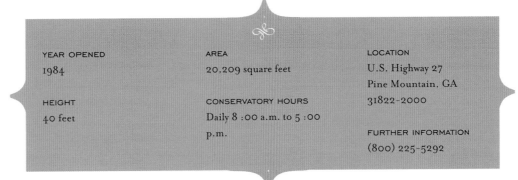

YEAR OPENED
1984

HEIGHT
40 feet

AREA
20,209 square feet

CONSERVATORY HOURS
Daily 8 :00 a.m. to 5 :00 p.m.

LOCATION
U.S. Highway 27
Pine Mountain, GA
31822-2000

FURTHER INFORMATION
(800) 225-5292

Crystal Bridge Tropical Conservatory

MYRIAD BOTANICAL GARDENS, OKLAHOMA CITY, OKLAHOMA

Myriad Botanical Gardens and the conservatory were the centerpiece of architect I.M. Pei's 1960s plan to revitalize Oklahoma City. For twenty years the Crystal Bridge Conservatory remained a dream, chiefly because the actual bids for the unusual structure were so much higher than Pei's original cost estimates. From the round tri-cord trusses that form the frame to the double-skinned Exolite™ acrylic glazing, almost everything about the conservatory required specialized technology.

Finally, in 1988, the Crystal Bridge Conservatory, designed by Conklin Rossant Architects of New York City, opened to the public. Due to the unusual spatial arrangement, one of the conservatory's best features is an elevated skywalk that brings visitors into the canopy and opens up views of the glorious plant collection from above. The focal point of the entire presentation is a thirty-five-foot waterfall that cascades magnificently into a small pool, filling the building with a low-amplitude roar.

Complementing this scene, the garden hosts a variety of fauna, including a population of Zebra Longwing butterflies that hatch at a rate of five thousand per year and fly freely around the conservatory. Two species of small anole lizards crawl in and around dry rock formations, while fish, frogs, and other amphibians enjoy the water features and humid conditions amidst the tropical plants. Overhead, lovebirds and

OPPOSITE: *Literally a crystal bridge, the conservatory spans a 1.5-acre lake fed by a natural aquifer that runs twenty-two feet below street level.*

ABOVE: *Oklahoma City's down-town conservatory sits in the midst of the seventeen-acre Myriad Botanical Gardens.*

OPPOSITE, LEFT: *Early construction photos reveal how "mountains" were built at each end of the conservatory.*

OPPOSITE, RIGHT: *Note the angled twin palms almost hidden by foliage, compared to their early days in the previous photograph.*

The conservatory and gardens provide vital greenery in the middle of the city.

parrots add to the atmosphere and provide sound effects.

The conservatory exhibits two distinct climates: the south end displays lush rainforest and humidity-loving tropical plants; the north end represents the dry tropics such as South Africa, Madagascar, and portions of Central and South America. Both ends have lavishly planted forty-foot-high mountains from which visitors can view the expanse. The realistic appearance of the mountains was created by applying silicone latex onto nearby rock outcroppings. The latex was used to fabricate molds for forty 100-square-foot sections that were then installed on top of reinforced steel angle iron. Against the backdrop, six specific collections stand out: the palms, which range from a tiny *Trachycarpus palmae* to the enormous Zombi palm (*Zombia antillarium*); a world-class selection of gingers,

orchids, bromeliads, begonias, and a large group of cycads, including the ancient *Encepholaratos altensteinii*, notable for its impressive eighteen-inch cone.

At the north and south end lobbies of the cylinder, sculpture artist Paula Collins created brick wall murals out of three-dimensional, hand-carved bricks pieced together and depicting a tropical plant theme. The flora on the brick, modeled after plants in the conservatory, were colored with ceramic stains.

Viewed from within the city, the Crystal Bridge's simple geometry makes a strong contribution to the skyline, providing a distinctively late-modernist statement. Within the structure, however, the conservatory's bold presence is softened by the enveloping horticultural experience, as the landscape and architecture engage in a showy dance of form and color.

YEAR OPENED	CONSERVATORY HOURS	LOCATION	FURTHER INFORMATION
1988	Monday–Saturday 9:00 a.m. to 6:00 p.m.; Sunday Noon to 6:00 p.m.; Closed Thanksgiving Day, Christmas Day, and New Year's Day	Reno and Robinson Avenues Oklahoma City, OK 73102	(405) 297-3995 www.okccityhall.org/ BotanicalGardens
HEIGHT			
70 feet			
AREA			
13,000 square feet			

Steinhardt Conservatory

BROOKLYN BOTANIC GARDEN, BROOKLYN, NEW YORK

The Steinhardt Conservatory occupies a complex of five buildings, including the historic Palm House designed by McKim, Mead & White at the turn of the century. The original Palm House, no longer open to the public, serves as a serene reminder of the Garden's beginnings and as a support greenhouse for conservatory displays. The new Steinhardt Conservatory winds through three pavilions—octagonal glass silos above ground, connected by subterranean rooms. Davis, Brody & Associates designed the new buildings partly below ground, giving the visitor a sense of emerging into each individual display room in a moment of discovery.

Visitors enter the pavilions through the central 245-foot rectangular glasshouse containing the Trail of Evolution complete with fossils, rock formations, and early examples of plant life like cycads. At one end is the impressive Aquatic House with both a shallow pool of tropical plants and a deep-water aquarium that one can view from below as well as above. Along the wall, two glass cases hold selected orchids and a bog display of insectivores. At the other end of this large building lies the outstanding C.V. Starr Bonsai Museum, full of meticulously trained specimens like the majestic four-hundred-year-old white pine tree. A central staircase separates the two halves of the building and leads underground to a sky-lit area with changing art exhibits and a cafeteria.

OPPOSITE: *Exterior views of the Steinhardt Conservatory show only the glass silos, concealing lower-level rooms and passages under restful grass, ponds, and terraces.*

Steinhardt highlights water gardens,
both inside and out.

ABOVE: *Centuries-old specimens in the majestic C.V. Starr Bonsai Museum within the Steinhardt Conservatory. The foreground water table display in the Japanese Suiban tradition enhances the presentation.*

LEFT: *Steinhardt's rockwork, in naturalistic formations, highlights plants in two of the three buildings.*

ABOVE: *Pictorial storyboards run in front of exhibits to explain every phase of plants, from exploration and conservation to man's use and abuse of them.*

RIGHT: *Exotic bulb display in the Helen Mattin Warm Temperate exhibition area.*

Below ground, visitors can enter the three pavilions, each of which is devoted to a separate ecosystem. Towering palms and a lush tapestry of jungle flora enhance the Tropical Rainforest Pavilion. A gradual ramp around the perimeter provides a changing view of a sample ecosystem from a variety of perspectives, including from within the canopy—a rarity in most conservatories. The Helen Mattin Warm Temperate Pavilion showcases a collection of popular plants from regions of the world with similar growing conditions—including eastern Asia, Australia, and New Zealand, the western coasts of the Americas, southern Africa, and the Mediterranean—allowing for meaningful comparisons. The Desert Pavilion contains North African and Sonoran succulents and American cacti, as well as a hot humid room with coffee plants and citrus trees.

Directly beneath the Aquatic House, where the deep water aquarium dips into the subterranean space, lies a busy children's area. The exhibit, called Amazing Plants, reflects Brooklyn Botanic Garden's commitment to the Metropolitan Plant Project, a botanical education concept for understanding plants. The goal is to teach people about the kind of plants that naturally grow in their urban neighborhoods as well as around the world. In Amazing Plants, a dandelion receives as much emphasis as a rose or a street tree. Interactive games, simple storyboards, and focused activities promote the idea that if people understand their place in nature and the significance of plants in their own lives, they will not only care for plants in their neighborhoods but will also realize the significance of endangered species across the globe. This concept repeats itself in more adult-oriented displays throughout the conservatory.

In the middle of New York, the Steinhardt Conservatory presents a warm, inviting, and friendly atmosphere in which to learn about plants, whether they are sitting in pots on the windowsill or found deep within tropical jungles.

YEAR OPENED
1988

HEIGHT
65 feet

AREA
24,000 square feet

CONSERVATORY HOURS
Tuesday–Friday 8:00 a.m. to 6:00 p.m., Weekends and holidays 10:00 a.m. to 6:00 p.m., April–September; Tuesday–Friday 8:00 a.m. to 4:30 p.m., Weekends and holidays 10:00 a.m. to 4:30 p.m., October–March; Closed Mondays except public holidays; Also closed Thanksgiving Day, Christmas Day, and New Year's Day

LOCATION
1000 Washington Avenue Brooklyn, NY 11225

FURTHER INFORMATION
(718) 623-7200
www.bbg.org

The Lucille Halsell Conservatory

SAN ANTONIO BOTANICAL GARDEN, SAN ANTONIO, TEXAS

In San Antonio, international designer Emilio Ambasz and local architect Jones & Kell teamed up to create a contemporary conservatory that breaks with tradition in several important ways. The five different pavilions are not interconnected; each has its own entrance from a central open air courtyard. The exhibit rooms, in turn, are sunk below ground, and the biggest have individually designed pyramidal ceilings that rise as striking, unusual sculptural elements in the landscape. All the mechanical rooms, offices, and back-up areas are also underground, which helps impart a cooling advantage during the intense Texas summers.

The subterranean design succeeds best in the Alpine Room. Though many have tried, very few conservatories in the United States can maintain healthy alpine plants that require cool soil in addition to cool water and air. This fine alpine collection grows under totally artificial conditions in a chamber that resembles a Wardian case, the kind of terrarium-type transport container invented by ninetennth-century plant explorers. Computerized climate control features within the box mimic mountainous conditions, with fourteen hours of sunlight during the growing season and only eight hours of dim light during dormancy. Two refrigeration systems provide cool air and chill the coils that run six inches under the soil level. A dehumidifier keeps the plants from rotting in the winter.

OPPOSITE: *Even though it looks airy, the Lucille Halsell Conservatory contains enough steel and concrete to build a thirty-story building.*

{137}

*Visitors can also view
the dense foliage of the Palm House
from a winding staircase
and an elevated catwalk above.*

*The conservatory's upper glass is
the only feature discernable from a
distance.*

ABOVE: *One of the best epiphyte exhibits, this room shows the full range of epiphytic plants and growing conditions.*
RIGHT: *Temperatures in the cooled Alpine Room of high-altitude plants range from 34 to 60 degrees.*

The towering Palm House starts twenty feet below the surface, and the tropical palms, cycads, and a collection of palms suitable for San Antonio's subtropical climate rise to sixty-five feet, higher than in any other house in the garden. A winding staircase and elevated catwalk help visitors view the dense foliage from above. In contrast, the Desert Pavilion offers dry arroyos and small craggy hills adorned with cacti, succulents and the few trees that evolve in dry climates. Carefully chosen plants demonstrate their adaptability to dry conditions in three ways: evading the drought by going dormant during the dry season, enduring the period of no water by storing it in fleshy leaves and interior channels, or by developing a quicktime life cycle that takes place entirely during the brief periods of desert rain.

Misty with fog and overflowing with ferns, aroids, insectivores, and tropical vines, the Fern Room nestles twenty-three feet below ground level. A flat glass roof is partially shaded to protect the plants from the searing Texas sun. A Hot Tropical Room embraces the rich variety of plants that flourish in the hot and humid rainforest. The final pavilion houses an Exhibition Room containing primarily epiphytes, orchids, bromeliads, and other tropicals, many of which grow on a large artificial tree, realistically covered with cork oak bark. On the far corner of the Exhibition Room, thirty tons of volcanic rock show off lithophyte plants that get their nutrients from the air but grow on rocks. The display, complete with tiny waterfalls trickling down the twelve-foot-tall wall of stone, provides an interesting addition to the traditional epiphyte displays.

The outdoor courtyard hub of the Halsell Conservatory contains a pond filled with massive Amazon lily pads, *Victoria cruziana*, the kind favored by Victorian conservatories. Visitors see the water display each time they enter and exit the exhibits, strolling a total of four miles of guided pathway. The total effect is that of a proud conservatory of the future giving a curious nod the tradition from which it evolved.

YEAR OPENED
1988

HEIGHT
65 feet

AREA
18,000 square feet

CONSERVATORY HOURS
Daily 9 :00 a.m. to 6 :00 p.m., March–October; 8 :00 a.m. to 5 :00 p.m., November–February; Open until 9 :00 p.m. on Thursday evenings, June–August; Closed Christmas Day and New Year's Day

LOCATION
555 Funston Place
San Antonio, TX 78209

FURTHER INFORMATION
(210) 207-3255
www.sabot.org

The Dorothy Chapman Fuqua Conservatory

ATLANTA BOTANICAL GARDEN, ATLANTA, GEORGIA

*T*he Dorothy Chapman Fuqua Conservatory is a tribute to the energy and vision of Atlanta Botanical Garden's former director, Ann Crammond, and the generosity of garden donor J.B. Fuqua in honor of his wife. After traveling the United States to visit the best glasshouses in the country, Crammond and the Fuquas delineated the elements they thought most appropriate to achieve the Atlanta Botanical Garden's mission of "display, education, research, conservation, and enjoyment." They worked with Heery Architects & Engineers, based in Atlanta. The result is a contemporary rotunda made of steel, glass, and rose-colored precast concrete, packed with carefully chosen plants that are considered sensitive, rare, threatened or endangered.

From exciting exhibits up front to high tech systems that operate in the background, they created a masterpiece. In the main lobby, terrariums teeming with poison dart frogs capture the imagination of all ages. Once inside the Tropical House, visitors are engulfed by an epiphyte display. They then walk through an orchid exhibit that illustrates the evolution of modern plants from primitive cycads and ferns up to modern flowering hybrids. Nearly one thousand species orchids go on rotational display, so the public sees only a few at a time, such as *Coryanthes*, which grows exclusively in ant nests in the wild. In the densely planted dome a fourteen-foot waterfall cascades over lava rock and a fogging system sprays mist at

OPPOSITE: *The Dorothy Chapman Fuqua Conservatory helped expand the mission of the Atlanta Botanical Garden to include conservation.*

*Palms, the backbone of
conservatories, provide food, shelter,
clothing, oil for candy and cosmetics,
and much more.*

ABOVE: *A dwarf conifer collection surrounds the back of the conservatory.*

LEFT: *In its native Sumatra, the* **Amorphophallus** titanum *grows on the west side of volcanic hillsides; the plant's lifecycle alternates from a bloom one year to a giant leaf the next.*

ABOVE: *A bird's-eye view of the tropical rotunda shows how one way paths lead visitors through the exhibits.*
RIGHT: *Red eye tree frogs and poison dart frogs warn predators away with brilliant colors that suggest bitterness or poison. The red eye frogs grow up to 4" long, while the poison dart frogs can be as tiny as ¾" when fully grown.*

frequent intervals, creating a primordial setting for unusual species from Madagascar
and the Seychelle and Mascarene Islands, all
located in the Indian Ocean. To complete
the picture, insect-eating lizards and free-
flying birds add sound and movement to the
jungle atmosphere.

The adjacent Desert House features Old
World succulents, focusing primarily on
those of the southwestern region of Madagascar where so many rare species still exist.
(Eighty-five percent of the island's 12,000
species grow nowhere else in the world.)
There are no cacti. Instead visitors revel in
the wonderful natural architecture of
euphorbias, asclepiads, aloes, welwitschia,
lithops, and mesembs—a magnificent diversity enclosed under one roof.

Specialty collections appear on a rotating
basis, reflecting the institution's conservation emphasis. Of particular interest are bog
plants, hardy and tropical carnivores, and
natives from the surrounding region. The
largest carnivorous pitcher plant on display is
the *Nepenthes truncata*, with a five-inch-wide
opening to lure insects, beetles, roaches, and
even unsuspecting lizards and frogs.

The newest building is an amazing orchid
complex, decked out with the latest climate
and lighting controls. The High-Tech Cor-
ridor between the existing tropical rotunda
and the new addition interprets the conservatory's species orchid collection to visitors,
explaining how they grow in the wild. One
part of the new building is devoted to tropical orchids and organized as a formal garden.
Another is designed as a jungle display in a
more naturalistic vein. Yet another special
section contains rare high altitude orchids
from the Tepui mountains of Brazil and
Venezuela, the Andean Region, and Southeast Asia.

The Atlanta Botanical Garden has
evolved into a major research institution,
and a visit to the Conservation Center shows
the classrooms, tissue culture lab, reference
room, and support greenhouses that make it
all possible.

YEAR OPENED
1989

HEIGHT
60 feet

AREA
29,000 square feet
(including Orchid Com-
plex, opening 2001)

CONSERVATORY HOURS
Tuesday–Sunday 10:00
a.m. to 6:00 p.m.;
Closed Thanksgiving
Day, Christmas Day, and
New Year's Day

LOCATION
1345 Piedmont Avenue
Atlanta, GA 30309

FURTHER INFORMATION
(404) 876-5859
www.atlantabotanical
garden.org

Bolz Conservatory

OLBRICH BOTANICAL GARDENS, MADISON, WISCONSIN

Bolz Conservatory's exterior design—a crystal pyramid topped by a geometric cupola—was inspired by the regional presence of Frank Lloyd Wright and the distinctive architecture of the Prairie School. The double-glazed construction uses clear tempered glass on the exterior and laminated glass on the interior, in conjunction with white fiberglass curtains on the south and west walls to protect against heat loss in the winter and excess heat from the summer sun.

Inside, the tropical setting contains approximately 750 plants, a twenty-foot-high waterfall and a flowing stream spanned by wooden bridges. Free-flying canaries, waxbills and diamond doves serve as an essential part of the building's Integrated Pest Management program by consuming insects. Staged exhibits emphasizing palms, aroids and epiphytes look like regular landscapes, but they display only one example of each species, instead of the massed arrangements and high density plantscapes seen in traditional conservatories. Recent Olbrich plant collecting expeditions to Ecuador and Belize garnered unusual specimens like Bullhoof (*Drypetes brownii*), notable because its new leaves emerge in a shocking metallic blue.

The southeast corner of the building glows with an Orchid Aerie. Using the gunnite process, craftsmen simulated a rock wall of fiberglass and concrete by casting limestone outcroppings in a nearby park. Orchids in full flower adorn the rock

OPPOSITE: *Only fifty feet high, Bolz Conservatory is joined to an existing educational complex of native stone.*

{149}

*Bolz Conservatory's functional shape
helps protect plants and people from
cold Northern winters.*

ABOVE: *Two hundred and twenty high-pressure misters keep the humidity above 60 percent and help counter the drying effects of winter heat.*

LEFT: *The Orchid Aerie, created of painted fiberglass and concrete, displays bromeliads, orchids, and other epiphytes brought out on a rotating basis from support houses.*

A bamboo arbor laden with tropical
plants adds to the jungle atmosphere.

wall that winds around to a greenhouse in back devoted solely to propagating the five hundred specimens in their orchid collection. Another popular plant display explores Foods of the Tropics, from carambola and guanabana to coffee, vanilla and breadfruit. Their area devoted to carnivores does an excellent job of showing the evolution of bog plants that grow in areas with so little nitrogen that the plants make up for the deficiency by consuming nitrogen-rich insects and small reptiles. Carnivores on display shows the plants' methods of trapping critters using sticky hairs, deep pitchers in which the prey drowns, and stiff leaves that clamp shut like those of the *Dionaea* or Venus flytrap. Eschewing modern computer controlled watering systems, the staff at Olbrich carefully waters everything by hand, using distilled water heated to 78 degrees.

Olbrich's Exploration Station is a recreated thatched research hut with an exhibit that reveals how rainforest plant materials decompose into soil. Inside the hut, a Snipping Garden opens on weekends for children to take home free plant cuttings in a mini-conservatory they make out of recycled plastic soda bottles.

Inch for inch, this relatively small conservatory rivals any in the country in terms of community devotion. Maybe it is because the place is a warm, fragrant oasis in the long Wisconsin winter, but annual attendance has more than tripled at Olbrich Botanical Gardens since the new conservatory was built. A full offering of educational and entertainment programs reaches out to all ages with engaging activities like the summer Butterfly Bonanza, the Holiday Flower and Train Show, and the family flashlight tour, in which visitors are taken into the tropical collection during the night to see how the jungle changes at night. For the casual visitor, a wide array of learning brochures and self-guided tour pamphlets appeal to specific age groups, starting with simple picture games, plant safaris and sensory exploration ideas for children as young as four years old.

YEAR OPENED
1991

HEIGHT
50 feet

AREA
10,000 square feet

CONSERVATORY HOURS
Monday–Saturday 10:00 a.m. to 4:00 p.m.; Sunday 10:00 a.m. to 5:00 p.m.; Closed Thanksgiving Day and Christmas Day

LOCATION
3330 Atwood Avenue
Madison, WI 53704

FURTHER INFORMATION
(608) 246-4550
www.olbrich.org

Rio Grande Botanic Garden Conservatory

RIO GRANDE BOTANIC GARDEN, ALBUQUERQUE, NEW MEXICO

Albuquerque's conservatory deserves recognition not only for its innovative architecture, but also for deviating from the traditional tropical plant displays. The conservatory's mission is to educate visitors about regional plants that grow around them—and as a necessary complement, in this desert climate, to show them how to create attractive gardens with plants that require minimal watering.

The conservatory is divided into two large pavilions with towers roughly resembling pyramids. The first building contains plants that are appropriate to the surrounding New Mexican landscape with an emphasis on Mediterranean plants that can flourish naturally in the Rio Grande Valley. According to a local expert, a Mediterranean climate is really only "a desert waiting to happen," and the biomes represented in the garden include parts of California, South Africa, Australia, coastal Chile, and the Mediterranean Basin where the native flora get all their water during the winter rainy season, then no water from spring through fall.

The second pavilion features plants from the arid climates of the Sonora, Baja, and lower Chihuahua Deserts of North America. Organ pipe cactus (*Stenocereos thurbi*), Ferocactus, and Echinocactus are some of the large, barrel-shaped, nonbranching cacti that thrive here. Visitors are amazed at how the cacti look when planted in groups. The Boojum tree (*Fouquieria columnaris*), a native of

OPPOSITE: *The conservatory and the zoo are highlights of Albuquerque Biological Park.*

{155}

*Rock formations and desert flora
mimic the rugged
New Mexican terrain.*